What people are saying about …

Pass It On

"Those of us who work with kids and parent our own children have been waiting for a 'rite of passage' experience like this for years. I'm so excited for *Pass It On* because it combines a yearly experience from K through 12 with biblical, memorable experiences at each grade level. Start at any grade and each rite of passage will provide a special milestone and memory for your child. Parents must understand that if we want our kids to keep their faith, we need to have more faith conversations during their growing years. I'm excited to endorse something that is more than a book—it's a movement of God."

Doug Fields, author, speaker, and executive
director of Homeword's Center for Youth/
Family at Azusa Pacific University

"In *Pass It On*, Jim Burns and Jeremy Lee offer a creative resource for building a 'spiritual legacy' into the lives of our kids through intentional and regular lifelong rites of passage. As Arnold van Gennep first noticed (in 1909) that most cultures create opportunities and pathways for the young called 'rites of passage'—essentially 'passing from one room … [of life] to another' and ultimately reaching a new status—Jim and Jeremy have crafted specific experiences and symbols for families and church communities to nurture young people from the room of 'child/youth' to full participation as spiritual partners in God's household. This book celebrates the role of family and community, and helps parents lead their kids to realize their place as adopted children of God, as siblings with all of God's people. As Jim and Jeremy say, 'Reading this book is meant to be a life-changing experience.'"

Chap Clark, author of *Hurt 2.0: Inside the World of Today's Teenagers* and professor of Youth, Family, and Culture at Fuller Theological Seminary

"I have often been asked for a practical resource to help parents and churches build rites of passage into the lives of their children and youth. This is the book I've been waiting for! *Pass It On* offers an uncomplicated road map for marking every year between kindergarten and high school graduation with a celebration, a turning point, a timeless moment that anchors our children deeply in God's persistent presence in each chapter of their own stories."

Mark DeVries, author of *Family-Based Youth Ministry,* founder of Ministry Architects, and cofounder of Ministry Incubators

"When I see that Jim Burns has written a book, I know that it will be encouraging, practical, faithful, and born of personal experience. *Pass It On* doesn't disappoint. With his cowriter, Jeremy Lee, Jim has given us the kind of book that can help youth workers, CE directors, children's pastors, parents, or anyone else who wants to support families in their journey of sowing and nurturing faith in the next generations."

Dr. Duffy Robbins, professor of youth
ministry at Eastern University

"Jim Burns and Jeremy Lee have done something remarkable in *Pass It On*. This book will challenge, inspire, and encourage Christian parents to celebrate their children in incredible new ways."

Craig Gross, founder of XXXchurch.com
and author of *Touchy Subjects*

"In *Pass It On*, Jim Burns, a seasoned and highly relevant veteran in the zenith of his career, joins with Jeremy Lee, an innovative parent ministry leader, to offer salient and poignant principles necessary for navigating today's family terrain. Wisdom, combined with experience, is offered in this unique contribution in the unexplored area of creating rites of passage for a new generation of parents hungry to intentionally pass down faith to their children in a meaningful and memorable fashion. Every parent needs to read and consider the encouragement in this book!"

Michelle Anthony, author of *Spiritual Parenting*
and *Becoming a Spiritually Healthy Family*

"I've written books for teens and parents. I like my stuff, but none of it even comes close to the rich and powerful steps that Jim and Jeremy have written. My oldest child is just entering high school, and I've got a couple younger children too. This book will not be on my shelf, but it'll be on my desk, on my nightstand, and in my satchel. I'm keeping it close. Rights of passages matter, and I/we need this."

Dr. Lars Rood, author, speaker, writer,
pastor, professor, and father

"As a youth worker and father, I'm thrilled to pour into my kids through these Rites of Passage Experiences. We practice some of these ideas already, and I'm excited to add even more. I've read almost everything that Jim Burns has ever written, and you should too!"

Josh Griffin, high school pastor at
Saddleback Church and cofounder
of Download Youth Ministry

"Do you want to make a difference in the world for God? Do you want to expand His kingdom? Do you want to live out the Great Commission and make disciples of Jesus Christ? If God has blessed you with children, your call to make a difference begins with the immortal souls of the sons and daughters the Lord has entrusted to your care. Your Great Commission begins at home! Most Christian parents truly want to see their children love Jesus and follow Him. The problem is most Christian parents don't have any kind of spiritual training plan or strategy. *Pass It On* can help move you from being a parent with merely good intentions to a parent with a dynamic, Bible-driven plan to impress upon the hearts of your children a love for God! It is packed with powerful lessons and unforgettable family experiences that God can use to draw your children to Him. Now is the time to get equipped for your most important Christian ministry—shepherding the souls of your children."

Dr. Rob Rienow, founder of Visionary
Family Ministries (www.visionaryfam.com)

"Reading and putting into practice *Pass It On* will be a game changer for families and churches. This book is well written, practical, and is a definite must-read for parents and church leaders!"

Ryan Frank, CEO and publisher of
KidzMatter and vice president of Awana

"I've always been a huge fan of intentional rites of passage (as opposed to the nonintentional cultural rites most of our children and teens stumble through). This book, like none I've ever seen, provides practical and actionable rites—along with amazing insight—for every year of elementary, middle, and high school. It's an absolute wealth—a treasure trove—of hope and spiritual parenting. I will be recommending this book to lots of parents!"

Mark Oestreicher, partner in the Youth Cartel
and author of *A Parent's Guide to Understanding
Teenage Brains* and *Understanding Your Young Teen*

"With the culture speaking loudly into kids' lives 24-7, it's essential that we take every opportunity we can to walk with our children through every stage of childhood and adolescence, offering meaningful instruction and annual rituals of passage as they navigate the difficult road to adulthood. In *Pass It On*, Jim Burns and Jeremy Lee share practical ideas and suggestions to make this happen. Their suggestions will help you help your kids hear the still, small voice of God and His grand and glorious plan for their lives in the midst of a noisy world full of competing stories."

Walt Mueller, founder and president of the
Center for Parent/Youth Understanding

"Two of my favorite people came together to collaborate on a project that is long overdue. Both Jim and Jeremy have a passion that comes to fruition in a book that assists families (and faith communities) in creating environments where such rites of passage can organically occur. They have honored their intent to encourage parents to embrace their roles as spiritual patriarchs and matriarchs, and it feels as if they are more tour guides than authors. As a parent, the reader can feel as though they are coming alongside in order to assist in the faith journey of children and adolescents. Well done, friends."

Dr. Allen Jackson, professor of youth
education and collegiate ministry at New
Orleans Baptist Theological Seminary

"Most parents want to spend more time with their children and create lasting memories, but they simply don't know how; they feel unqualified and ill-prepared. And that's why I love *Pass It On*! Jim and Jeremy have created a wonderfully simple, yet powerful, tool to help parents engage with their children in meaningful ways. I can't recommend it more highly!"

Kurt Johnston, pastor to students
at Saddleback Church

"*Pass It On* touches parents in every stage of parenting and provides them with powerful and practical strategies to engage their kids in meaningful, spiritual dialogue. Every parent who recognizes the mandate to pass the faith on to their kids will find inspiration and tools in this book. Keep it on the bottom shelf and refer to it often!"

Dr. Scott Turansky, cofounder of the
National Center for Biblical Parenting

"I have respected the ministry of Jim Burns and Jeremy Lee for years, but *Pass It On* will definitely go down as one of their most impactful works. If you are a parent, pastor, or ministry leader who is committed to reaching the next generation, this book is truly a game changer! The Rites of Passage Experiences they introduce are certain to influence families in a powerful way!"

Brian Dollar, author of *I Blew It* and founder
of High Voltage Kids Ministry Resources

"*Pass It On* empowers this generation of parents to build their own legacy of faith for their children, regardless of what legacy they themselves were born into. This is an important tool for any parent at any stage."

Albert Tate, senior pastor at Fellowship
Monrovia, Southern California

"*Pass It On* is the road map and blueprint of how to leave a spiritual legacy for your family. Jim and Jeremy aren't writing in theory; these are men living and doing what they write, and they have given us practical glimpses into the legacy we can have for our own families.

After reading this truth laid out on a platter, parents can never again say, 'I didn't know what to do.'"

Brian Housman, author of *Tech Savvy Parenting*
and executive director of 360 Family

"What Jim and Jeremy have done is put a tool in the hands of parents to practically lead their kids spiritually. In an age when family is under assault as never before, to give parents a tool that is life giving is a great gift indeed. This book helps us, as parents, make the most of every season in the life of our children. The art of passing on our faith is an invitation to our kids to see Jesus as beautiful rather than useful. To have a tool that guides that conversation is much needed. I hope you will be as blessed by this book as I have been."

Sam Luce, global family pastor at
Redeemer Church, Utica, New York

Pass It On

JIM BURNS & JEREMY LEE

Pass It On

Building a Legacy of Faith for Your Children
through Practical and Memorable Experiences

David C Cook®

transforming lives together

PASS IT ON
Published by David C Cook
4050 Lee Vance View
Colorado Springs, CO 80918 U.S.A.

David C Cook Distribution Canada
55 Woodslee Avenue, Paris, Ontario, Canada N3L 3E5

David C Cook U.K., Kingsway Communications
Eastbourne, East Sussex BN23 6NT, England

LCCN 2015936249
ISBN 978-1-4347-0907-3
eISBN 978-0-7814-1371-8

© 2015 Jim Burns and Jeremy Lee

The Author is represented by and this book is published in association with the
literary agency of WordServe Literary Group, Ltd., www.wordserveliterary.com.

The Team: Alex Field, Carly Razo Lohrmann,
Amy Konyndyk, Helen Macdonald, Karen Athen
Cover Design: Nick Lee
Cover Photo: Shutterstock

Printed in the United States of America
First Edition 2015

1 2 3 4 5 6 7 8 9 10

070715

To Cathy Burns
You have lived through our daughters' rites of passage and
have been a faithful, consistent, and genuine role model.
What a privilege it is to share this life with you, raising
our children to be responsible adults who love God.

To Christy, Becca, and Heidi
I know for sure we haven't done it perfectly, but since
before you were born, Mom and I shared a goal of passing
our faith on to you, the next generation. I am proud
of each of you for who you are and what you do.

To Elisabeth Lee
You have taught me that the path we walk is not safe, but
the God we serve is. As I walk the path God has given
me, it fills me with such courage to watch you walk yours.
There is no question that God's greatest gift to me is the
partner with whom I journey through life. I love you.

To Campbell and Hudson
You are Warrior Poets. A beautiful picture of strength and
gentleness woven together. Campbell, you remind me of
Nehemiah from Scripture. You treasure justice and are the
kind of leader people enjoy following. Hudson, you remind
me of John the Baptist from Scripture. You are full of purpose
and passion, and you are not a slave to the opinions of others.
My prayer for both of you is that you will grow to believe the
only use for fear is to kindle your courage. I love you both.

CONTENTS

Part 1: Setting It Up

Part 2: Rites of Passage Experiences

Part 3: Finish Strong

Foreword

Parents need additional voices speaking truth into their parenting motives, styles, and strategies. As a father of two, I pray that my children grow into Jesus-loving, responsible adults. Every day I am impressing messages upon their hearts. They hear everything I say and see everything I do. More than likely, they will repeat what they see and hear in me. My first prayer is that I impress a love for the Lord upon them (Deut. 6:7). My second prayer is that they will mature into adults who take personal responsibility for their work and homes.

Our tendency today is to accelerate childhood milestones and delay adulthood milestones. When our children are young, we push them hard to be successful in athletics and academics. We want them to succeed. "Go, go, go. Run, run, run" is our charge. We have fallen for the faulty input/output theory of parenting that teaches "Whatever you put into a child is what you will get out of a child." That simply is not true.

In the tween years (typically ages ten through twelve), our kids take off. They begin the process of individualization and separation. I believe this is by design of Almighty God. Your child is becoming a little adult. It's at this stage that parents switch from acceleration to delay. Now, we don't want them to grow up too fast. This is very confusing for a child. It's kind of like spurring a horse to go while pulling back on the reins. You need to do one or the other.

Healthy parents recognize and embrace the milestones of childhood and adulthood. Rather than resisting and delaying, you create a plan for each age and milestone. That is exactly what Jim and Jeremy do in this book. They give us a game plan for the ages.

As a parent, I'm asking …

"At what age should I have the sex talk with my kids?"

"How much should I tell them and when?"

"When should I let my daughter date?"

"When, if ever, should I get my son a phone?"

"When should my child get a job?"

"How much screen time per day is appropriate for my child?"

"Is there a way to help my child accept her identity and body?"

Pass It On: Building a Legacy of Faith for Your Children through Practical and Memorable Experiences, by my friends Jim Burns and Jeremy Lee, is an additional voice in your home. Parenting is hard. That's a fact. This book validates so much of what you are struggling with as a parent and at the same time helps you navigate all of the different seasons of your home.

As soon as you think you have a handle on the season of life your child is in, it is over and you find yourself in a brand-new "I have no clue what to do" season. I like theory, but I love practical "keep it on the lower shelf" helps as a parent.

My wife, Amy, and I are planning rites of passage for our children. We are grateful for *Pass It On* and plan on using the topics, ceremonies, and passages to encourage and build up our children, Corynn (twelve) and Carson (ten), physically, emotionally, relationally, and spiritually.

I hope you will consider doing the same.

Blessings,

Ted Cunningham, founding pastor of Woodland Hills Family Church, Branson, Missouri, and author of Fun Loving You *and* The Power of Home

Acknowledgments

A special thank-you from Jim to:

Cindy Ward for your leadership, servant's heart, and beautiful spirit in which you go about your life and work.

Doug Fields for the remarkable friendship and ministry partnership we have had since you were in the youth group. You are one of the most talented human beings alive.

Andrew Accardy for believing in HomeWord and the mission of strong marriages, confident parents, empowered kids, and healthy leaders. You are a genius and a friend.

The incredible HomeWord board members, who on a regular basis give guidance, direction, and support to this most amazing mission. Bless you and thank you.

A special thank-you from Jeremy to:

Dr. Jim Burns, who is easily my first acknowledgment. This book wouldn't exist if you didn't lend me your reputation and trust me enough to partner on this project.

Heather Stoll for doing the lion's share of helping me organize my thoughts and create this book. Thank you, Heather, for your dedication to this project. You did such a great job with all of this. It would not have happened without you.

Carly Lohrmann for taking on the job of refining this book. Thank you for the care and attention to detail you brought to this project.

Carrie Partridge for helping me put together the initial book proposal and doing an amazing job with it. Carrie, I appreciate your work. Thank you!

This book was inspired by my website, ParentMinistry.net. Therefore, I want to acknowledge the team that makes the website work every day: Marianne Howard, Chad Howard, Jackie Haba, Michael Bayne, Chelsea Bayne, Shellie Hochstetler, Jill York, Dan Istvanik, Karl Huber, Brandon Wood, George Bewley, and Sarah Laws. They are servants who are unbelievably passionate about our mission of helping churches build an excellent parent ministry.

Introduction

Reading this book is meant to be a life-changing experience. One of the deepest desires of almost all Christian parents is to pass on a legacy of faith to our children. Our desire is there, our motives are there, but sometimes we don't know what to do. Frankly, some of us are just trying to get to Friday, and then we have to start all over again. At HomeWord we often say, "One of the major purposes of the church is to mentor parents; parents mentor their children, and the legacy of faith continues to the next generation." It's a great thought and not exactly easy.

Every family in the world has milestones and rites of passage that are important to celebrate, though few of us celebrate them with the kind of intentionality we wish we would. In *Pass It On*, we have given you a road map to celebrate certain milestones each year in your child's development. Jewish people celebrate boys' coming of age with bar mitzvahs and girls' religious maturity with bat mitzvahs—both beautiful rites of passage incorporating deep spiritual roots and blessings.

The goal of *Pass It On* is to give you as parents tools to celebrate rites of passage in each of your children's lives. We use symbols, experiences, and the community of believers around your child to give him or her a special day—or sometimes a special weekend—each year.

Here is what we promise:

- The experiences we suggest are special and not difficult to create.
- You won't need a theology degree to incorporate any of these rites of passage.
- These memorable and life-changing experiences are to be shared and enjoyed with your children.
- Your kids, no matter their ages, will understand that each of these rites of passage has special spiritual meaning that will enhance their faith.

Although we have created *Pass It On* rites of passage for every stage in school, you can start wherever you want. We know parents who have used some of the first rites of passage for older kids. We have also seen a lot of parents adapt our suggestions in other ways to fit their families.

Each Rite of Passage Experience chapter is filled with

- a *topic* you are celebrating and an explanation;
- a *ceremony* you can incorporate into the experience;
- a *symbol* you can give your child as a reminder of his or her milestone;
- a *testimony* of how another family celebrated this rite of passage;
- instructions on *wording* and *scriptures* corresponding with each celebration; and

- a *"what you need to know about [each grade level]"* at the end of each chapter to outline your child's developmental level physically, emotionally, relationally, and spiritually.

Pass It On is not meant to be a resource for all the subjects discussed in each rite of passage. There are plenty of other great books to take you deeper and further into these subjects. Rather, we created *Pass It On* to present an inspiring set of experiences to celebrate, as a family, certain important rites of passage in your child's life. We encourage you to dig deeper into many of these subjects and continue to talk about them as your child grows and matures.

For many years I have wanted to see a movement of Christian parents celebrating rites of passage with their children and families, and I have witnessed some very moving experiences with kids and the community of people who participated. I remember an evening I spent with Jeremy Lee in Nashville, Tennessee, where we spent the entire time talking about rites of passage and the great work he was doing at his church, which he later continued at ParentMinistry.net. This book was born out of our desire to be a part of what we believe is a movement of God in which parents are focusing more on celebrating the milestones of their children's faith and lives. We pray this book helps you along the way.

Blessings,
Jim Burns, PhD,
president of HomeWord and executive director of HomeWord
Center for Youth and Family at Azusa Pacific University

Before We Begin

Our society googles everything to try to understand it. I wish we could google "raising a child" and all the answers to help us become perfect parents would just pop up. Unfortunately, it doesn't work that way (we wish it did!). Raising a child is one of the most sacred responsibilities God will ever call most of us to. The beautiful part is that God walks with us through every step of the parenting journey. He never leaves us alone. Not once.

That's the feeling we hope you get when you read this book. We hope you feel that you are not alone. We hope to inspire, encourage, and spur you on to give your child the most important gift you'll ever give him or her: an understanding of and invitation to faith.

The first part of the book provides an explanation of what a rite of passage is and why it's important. The second part focuses on each year of a child's life, from kindergarten through twelfth grade. In each year, you'll learn about a shared spiritual experience called a rite of passage that you can lead your child through. We call this journey the Rite of Passage Experience.

As you read through each year, you'll see that we first introduce each rite of passage and then give you practical resources you can use while leading your child through the experience. We've tried to do as much of the work as possible so you can enjoy the moment with your child.

In many ways this book is like a reference book that you will come back to and visit each year. That's one of the things we love about it. We'll get to journey with you as you introduce faith to your child and "pass it on" to him or her.

Part 1

Setting It Up

1

A Legacy Moment

Imagine for a moment that you and your spouse are sitting in an estate attorney's office. It's time for you to prepare your will, and the first words out of the attorney's mouth are: "When you die, who would you like to receive your possessions?" You and your spouse probably point to each other.

The attorney then asks, "What if you both die?" Again, you are in agreement. "The kids."

For some it's a morbid thought, but the truth is inevitable: we will all die. And when we do, it is not only our physical possessions we'll leave behind. More important, we will leave our legacies. The spiritual riches passed on to our children far outweigh the value of any earthly inheritance—spiritual legacies remain for generations.

Most parents, including us, feel at times that the process of leaving a healthy, vibrant, life-transforming spiritual legacy is daunting. It is a most awesome task, yet when broken down to its basic foundation, although challenging, it's actually fairly simple.

You may feel ill-equipped to develop a spiritual legacy for your children and family, but the fact that you are reading this book shows you have already begun. The number one way to leave a spiritual legacy is to simply love your children, which quite obviously you *do*.

We know you do. That's why you are involved in their schools, take them to sports practices, attend decades of games or recitals, enroll in dance and gymnastic classes, arrange for music lessons, and shop at healthy food stores even when your kids seem as if they couldn't care less about nutrition. Clearly, you love them. In fact, there isn't anything you wouldn't do for them. We know, because we are parents too.

What would happen if you applied the same commitment, preparation, and discipline to your children's spiritual growth as you do to their education or athletic development?

Maybe you're thinking, *I take the kids to church, and the people at church know a lot more than I do* or *I haven't read the Bible from cover to cover* or *I don't have a seminary degree* or *I'm not a spiritual giant.*

What if we told you that God's original plan for passing on faith—leaving a spiritual legacy—rests in all parents' hands? What if we told you that by simply talking about faith in your home you can influence your child in an amazing way? In fact, studies have shown that young people who have faith conversations in their homes are much more likely to stay in church and adhere to their faith.[1]

If parents took developing spiritual legacies in their kids' lives as seriously as they do school, sports, and other activities, we believe the trajectory of families would change for generations to come. The premise of this book is that celebrating rites of passage moments will redefine faith formation for your kids and for your family. Celebrating those rites of passage can be simple, yet life transforming.

We often ask parents, "Were rites of passage celebrated in your home, and did your parents build a spiritual legacy?" Few respond that their parents were proactive in building legacy experiences, and even fewer tell us it was a regular part of their upbringing.

Well, we want to help change that for your family and your children.

The Bible teaches that we inherit consequences—good and bad—from previous generations of our families, even to the third and fourth generations. The choices, traditions, and teachings we offer our children will affect not only them but also their children.

Do you know the names of your great-great-great-grandparents? Few people do. But the truth is that you are affected by their lives, for better or worse. When you lay a spiritual foundation in the lives of your kids, you are influencing your grandchildren and great-grandchildren as well.

Meet the Edwards and the Jukes families.[2]

Jonathan Edwards was a famous speaker. He was a God-honoring man who faithfully served the Lord. He married a lovely woman named Sarah. Among the more than four hundred descendants of Jonathan and Sarah Edwards, there were fourteen college presidents, more than one hundred college professors, almost an equal number of lawyers, thirty judges, sixty physicians, at least sixty authors, and more than one hundred clergyman, missionaries, and theology professors. In the case of Jonathan and Sarah Edwards, we would say their spiritual influence was evident through many generations.

The second family was led by a man named Max Jukes. His two hundred eighty descendants included murderers, rapists, and prostitutes. Sixty were habitual thieves, fifty-five died of sexually transmitted diseases, and several spent much of their lives in prison. In 1877, Richard Louis Dugdale conducted the original study of the failure in morality exhibited by the Jukes family. Dugdale visited jails and prisons in upstate New York and was amazed to find inmates in prisons from all over the area who were from the same family tree. He ended up writing *The Jukes; a Study in Crime, Pauperism, Disease, and Heredity*, making this family famous for the exact opposite reason the Edwards family was. Some have said that in all of American history, few families rival that of Max Jukes's for immorality and corruption.

Max Jukes's influence was evident, like Jonathan Edwards's, but it was clearly not a legacy of faith.

Even if your family heritage more closely resembles the Jukeses than the Edwardses, you can begin to live your life as the *transitional generation*. A transitional generation parent works hard to *recover* from the sins of the past, rather than *repeat* them. Part of that happens by changing the direction of your family's spiritual legacy. You really are a spiritual patriarch or matriarch, and we want to challenge you to operate on that vision and rise to that job description. When you face difficult days, focus on the image of your legacy.

All of this leads to one amazing truth: what you do today matters. Every moment of your parenting journey will influence your children, grandchildren, and great-grandchildren.

In building a legacy for your children, you are helping them become responsible adults who love God. You can build lasting traditions and experiences that will matter long after you are gone. This book will teach you how to help your kids find the three Ms: *mission, mate,* and *Master*.

First, we believe that all of us were put on earth for a *mission*. Each person's mission and purpose are unique. Passing on your faith and celebrating rites of passage will help your children find their missions and teach them how to integrate their purposes into everyday living.

The second *m* is *mate*. Who your children marry will directly affect all aspects of their lives. Many of us would love to pick our children's husbands or wives, but if you live in the Western world, that probably isn't going to happen. However, you can help your children mature into the kinds of men and women who will choose their spouses well and build positive, healthy marriages and families.

Ultimately this rites of passage book is all about the third *m*: developing a relationship with the *Master*. A right relationship with Jesus Christ meets the deepest need of humankind. Studies tell us that 64 percent of the people who make a commitment to Jesus Christ do so before age eighteen.[3]

Each experience in this book will help you and your kids identify Christ's presence at major passages in their lives. Nothing is perfect on this side of heaven, yet adults who live within the will of God and have a mission, mate, and Master are building inheritances with eternal value.

2

God's Blueprint

The idea of passing on one's faith can be intimidating, and the realization that a child's view of God comes from what he or she receives (and perceives) at home makes most parents cringe. Frankly, there have been times in our own lives when that reality has been downright terrifying.

When faced with the task of passing on their faith, parents tend to respond in one of five ways. They

1. become paralyzed, so they ignore it and do nothing;
2. overcompensate and do more than needed;
3. select a book, give it to their child, and hope he or she figures it out;
4. delegate the task to someone else, and hope it works out for the best; or
5. understand the vital role parents have in the life of their child and strategically pass on faith to him or her.

What if we told you the blueprint for passing on faith has already been designed? God gave it to us in the Bible, and He provides very specific instructions on how to leave a spiritual legacy.

The rest of this book will teach you how to take God's blueprint for passing on faith and build a strategic plan for infusing faith into every year of your child's life.

Pretty exciting, isn't it? As we said in chapter 1, it's both simple and challenging.

Many biblical scholars regard Deuteronomy—and chapter 6 in particular—as the thesis statement of the entire Old Testament. Even today it is understood as the purpose and plan of the Hebrew people. It has been that way since the days of Moses. This blueprint is known as the Shema, meaning "to listen" in Hebrew. It is found in Deuteronomy 6:4–9.

> Hear, O Israel: The LORD our God, the LORD is one. Love the LORD your God with all your heart and with all your soul and with all your strength. These commandments that I give you today are to be on your hearts. Impress them on your children. Talk about them when you sit at home and when you walk along the road, when you lie down and when you get up. Tie them as symbols on your hands and bind them on your foreheads. Write them on the doorframes of your houses and on your gates.

There is a three-point purpose in these words:

1. Faithfulness and fidelity (loyalty) to God (Deut. 6:4–5)
2. Transmission of faith and love to children (Deut. 6:6–7)
3. Constant mindfulness of the teachings and presence of God (Deut. 6:8–9)

These three points are the road map to passing on faith. Your family commits to living a life of loyalty to God. You love Him with everything you have and with all your strength (Deut. 6:4–5). As you live out your faith to the best of your ability, you impress faith upon the hearts of your children (Deut. 6:6–7). Finally, you bring the presence of God into the lives of your kids by allowing the presence of God to be integral to your everyday activities (Deut. 6:8–9).

We are to be proactive and intentional about our faith, which is why celebrating rites of passage becomes a vital part of the parenting process.

The Shema is the most-often quoted scripture in the Bible and is recited every morning and evening in Orthodox Jewish homes. When the Shema is quoted on the Sabbath at a synagogue, the congregation stands. Imagine Mary holding her baby, Jesus, in her arms and reciting this scripture to Him every day from the time He was born!

Jewish parents understood and took seriously the challenge of passing their faith on to their children. But the modern-day church has in some ways missed this opportunity, because too many parents, even well-meaning ones, have delegated the teaching of faith to the church. Parents and the church should work together to instill faith and God-honoring values in our kids. It's not an either/or; it's both—with parents taking the primary leadership role.

When parents understand their roles in passing on legacies of faith to their children, they don't have to think of this task as a burden; it is, instead, one of the major goals and privileges of raising children.

Ultimately, children must make their own faith decisions. And they are much more likely to do so when influenced by a parent who speaks and lives out faith in the home. There is something special about the love between a mother or father and a child. In fact, there is no greater influence in the life of a child than a parent.

Isn't it incredible that the God who created the heart of a child to crave the attention of his or her parents also selected those parents to be the primary spiritual influencers in his or her life? It is an amazing, humbling, and encouraging thought.

God did not stop with that directive, though. Consider the final verses of the Shema:

> Tie them as symbols on your hands and bind them
> on your foreheads. Write them on the doorframes
> of your houses and on your gates.

These verses highlight the fact that part of God's plan for passing on faith is the use of symbols and ceremonies to reinforce beliefs. Most parents have not considered how important symbols and ceremonies are to the transmission of faith, but God uses them throughout Scripture to share His message.

Have you ever visited Washington, DC? It is a city filled with symbols and monuments. You can visit the Lincoln Memorial, the

Washington Monument, the Vietnam Veterans Memorial, and the Jefferson Memorial. You can witness the changing of the guard at the Tomb of the Unknown Soldier or attend a session of Congress.

Those symbols and ceremonies remind Americans of our heritage of freedom and the sacrifices made for that freedom. They are a testimony of all that makes America great. Even when people sit on opposite sides of the political aisle, these monuments remind us of the values that led to our country's founding. They are a call to something greater than ourselves.

Symbols are objects that have special meaning attached to them. If we visited your home and asked your child to take us on a tour, he or she would no doubt show us pictures, letters, heirlooms, art, souvenirs, and other symbols that not only tell your family's story but also explain what is most important to you. Symbols have power, and they are a special way to help children understand abstract concepts of faith and spirituality.

God calls His people to use symbols and ceremonies to remember or commemorate significant moments in their lives.

Think back to the Old Testament. Jacob set up a memorial at Bethel (Gen. 28), Jacob and Laban erected an altar at Gilead (Gen. 31), and Joshua built a memorial as the Israelites entered the Promised Land (Josh. 4). Once the nation of Israel was established, God instituted ceremonies:

- Passover
- The Festival of Tabernacles
- The Feast of Firstfruits
- The Feast of Unleavened Bread

- The Feast of Trumpets
- The Feast of Atonement
- Pentecost

The purpose of these ceremonies was to provide concrete reminders to reflect on God's provision. God instituted portions of each of these occasions specifically to include children.

We've both participated in a few of these Jewish celebrations, and during the portions where parents address their children on topics of faith, the beautiful traditions remind children of a God-moment in history and in their own lives.

When you understand the context of the Old Testament, it becomes clear that God thinks generationally. He set up rituals, ceremonies, and symbols that gave a system for parents and communities to pass on faith to their children. That is God's ideal scenario for someone to receive His story. A parent teaching a child was His original plan.

This is not just an Old Testament principle, though. When Jesus began His earthly ministry, He used imagery and parables (symbols) to communicate truth. He was baptized (ceremony), and He used wine and bread (symbols) in the Passover meal (ceremony) to teach about His crucifixion and resurrection. In fact, baptism and communion are two ordinances of the church still practiced today.

In the Shema, it says to "tie them [God's commandments] as symbols on your hands and bind them on your foreheads." Many Orthodox Jews take this directive literally. A phylactery is a small container that holds a parchment of Scripture from the Torah. Worn on the forehead or forearm, it is a tangible interpretation of verse 8 from Deuteronomy 6. In the same way, Jews also instituted the mezuzah. This small box with written verses in it is attached or hung on the right side of door-posts and gates in Jewish homes and communities and serves as a visible reminder of their identity as God's chosen people.

As a modern-day Christian, you are not commanded to wear a phylactery or hang a mezuzah on your door. However, you are given the great privilege and responsibility of impressing God's truth on the hearts of your children. God created children with concrete minds. That means they learn best with actual objects and events, rather than concepts and generalizations. Using symbols and ceremonies helps children understand and celebrate their faith.

The ultimate purpose of this book is to encourage parents to embrace their roles as spiritual patriarchs and matriarchs. God has called you to take your children on a journey to discover who He is by illustrating what faith in Him looks like. By infusing faith into your everyday life, you can reinforce the truths taught during each annual Rite of Passage Experience.

So there you have it. God's blueprint for passing down faith looks like this:

- Parents serve as the primary spiritual leaders in a family.
- Passing on faith is meant to take place in the everyday rhythm of life.
- Symbols and ceremonies are important tools for helping children understand God's story.

Now we are ready to learn how the Rites of Passage Experiences can help you put this blueprint into action.

3

What Is a Rite of Passage Experience?

One of the rites of passage for the Burns family was when my wife, Cathy, took each of our daughters away for an overnight trip when they were eleven years old to read and discuss a book about healthy, God-honoring sexuality. The twenty-four-hour trip was geared for good dialogue and fun. They went out for a fun meal, bought a new outfit, and generally did fun girl stuff along with the sex education experience.

At age sixteen, the first date our girls had was with me. I took each one out to a fancy dinner, bought her an outfit (more of a love language for girls than guys), and presented her with the opportunity to commit to the Purity Code: *In honor of God, my family, and my future spouse, I commit to sexual purity.* I then helped her pick out a purity ring as a symbol of her commitment.

What we found with both of these rites of passage is that each daughter's experience and response was a bit different, but still a special reminder of God's presence, even in the relational side of their lives. Rites of passage tend to be reminders that His story is also a part of your family's story.

Rites of Passage Experiences comprise a thirteen-year series of shared spiritual moments between parent and child that use the power of symbols and ceremonies to infuse faith into the natural transitions that take place in a child's life.

They are those special moments when you reach for the camera, invite friends over to join you, buy gifts to celebrate, shed a tear, or just throw a huge party. It's usually in those moments that you find yourself saying out loud, "They are growing up so fast."

So often we let these times come and go, and in doing so miss a great chance to leverage the moment to pass on faith. You don't have to ever miss that opportunity again. Each year, from kindergarten through high school graduation, you and your child can participate in one faith-based Rite of Passage Experience.

We've chosen to use each grade level as a time to introduce a different rite of passage. The grade level is more of a guideline than an absolute. If you don't start this when your child is in kindergarten (and many parents don't), just pick up at whatever grade level your child is currently and then look back at some of the other Rites of Passage Experiences and do the ones you think might still benefit your child.

Some have asked why there is only one experience each year. The goal of each Rite of Passage Experience is to inspire you and help you understand the needs of your child at each age. As you will see, each experience contains key spiritual truths as well as practical skills your child should learn. You will be instilling and reinforcing those throughout the year. Our hope is that as you go, God will give you more ideas of how to use symbols and ceremonies to infuse faith into the everyday moments of your life.

But we don't want to make these rites of passage practices overwhelming. One great experience each year is better (and more memorable) than numerous mediocre experiences.

Part 2 is divided into thirteen chapters—one for each year of school from kindergarten through twelfth grade. Each year, your child will be invited to participate in a rite of passage to celebrate a value or commemorate a milestone:

- Kindergarten: An Invitation to Generosity
- First Grade: An Invitation to Responsibility
- Second Grade: An Invitation to the Bible
- Third Grade: An Invitation to Rhythm
- Fourth Grade: An Invitation to Friendship
- Fifth Grade: An Invitation to Identity
- Sixth Grade: Preparing for Adolescence
- Seventh Grade: The Blessing
- Eighth Grade: Purity Code Weekend
- Ninth Grade: Driving Contract
- Tenth Grade: Money Matters
- Eleventh Grade: Family Tree
- Twelfth Grade: Manhood/Womanhood Ceremony

Although specific grades are assigned to each rite of passage, consider them to be guidelines or suggestions. Certain experiences might need to be repeated so you can let the truths sink in. Others may already be a part of your family rhythm. If you see a rite of passage that fits perfectly for your child right now, go ahead and experience it with him or her. God will inspire you, as the parent, to lead your child through this process in a way that fits perfectly for your family. We like to call this "personally tailored discipleship." Each child and each family will look at these experiences a bit differently, which is healthy.

We have worked with hundreds of families who have carried out the Rites of Passage Experiences in their home. Let us share some advice for the journey ahead of you:

- *Adjust your expectations.* If you expect a certain reaction from your child or teenager during a Rite of Passage Experience, you might be disappointed. Decide ahead of time that this is much more about you carrying out your mission from God to pass on faith than getting your child to have a certain reaction.

- *Something is better than nothing.* Life gets busy. Most of the Rites of Passage Experiences can be completed in one or two evenings. This is intentional because we know how hard it is to carve out time. If you are going through a crazy season, don't try to make this into a Hollywood production. Do what *your* time and budget allow to make the experience as memorable as possible.

- *Awkwardness is the gateway to intimacy.* The Rites of Passage Experiences can create intimate moments, but intimacy is often on the other side of awkwardness. You might have to push

through some awkwardness with your child,
but the reward of intimacy is totally worth it.

- *Younger siblings are watching.* If you do a Rite
of Passage Experience with an older sibling, be
prepared to carry it out for the younger sibling
when the younger child reaches the same age.

No matter how you proceed through this book, we are going to
be with you every step of the way. More important, as you seek to
instill faith in the life of your home, we believe God will instruct,
equip, and bless your efforts. You are following God's blueprint by
using symbols and ceremonies to pass on faith in your home. By
taking your child on a journey to discover who God is, He is going to
show up in ways you never could have imagined. You will be amazed
to see what happens when you follow His lead.

Part 2

Rites of Passage Experiences

1

Kindergarten: An Invitation to Generosity

Kindergarten naturally introduces children to a greater level of independence, which can simultaneously elicit fear and pride in parents. Fear because of the potential for negative influences entering a child's life, but pride because the child is becoming more independent and responsible. Many parents tell us that the first day of kindergarten holds deep joy mixed with a little sadness—it certainly did for us.

It's important to guard against allowing your world to revolve around your child once he reaches this milestone and steps further into the world outside of home. A child who believes the world revolves around him is in danger of developing a sense of entitlement and a me-focused attitude—both of which are the enemies of generosity. But you have the opportunity to influence and shape your child in powerful ways as he begins this journey into adulthood.

Instead of holding on more tightly and trying to insulate your child from the influences of the world, what if you used his newfound independence to teach him about the needs of others? What if you looked not just at his size but also at his potential to influence this world for good? What if you participated in a project designed to awaken a servant's heart within him? It would be an amazing beginning to a lifelong faith journey, and kindergarten is the perfect place to start.

Entitlement is a real battle for children in today's world. It's challenging to protect them from feeling that they deserve everything they want, but there's a simple antidote to entitlement: service. It's never too early to help children look outside of themselves and discover what it is like to share the love of Jesus Christ with others. After all, the call to Christ is the call to serve.

Something special happens when a family serves together. I (Jeremy) will never forget talking to a dad after he and his family returned from a mission trip. "We could have taken twenty trips to Disney World and never experienced the type of closeness I felt serving with my family on this mission trip," he told me.

A beautiful fellowship takes place when a family serves together, and it's in that setting you can invite your kindergartner to learn generosity.

Kindergarten Rite of Passage
Ceremony: Family service project
Symbol: Framed family photograph
from service project

Have you thought about what you are going to buy your child for Christmas? It's probably getting more difficult to think of something he really needs, because by the time most kids reach the age of five or six, they've accumulated so much stuff from Christmas gifts, Easter baskets, and birthday bashes, they barely have time to play with it all or they're so overwhelmed they can't decide what to reach for. Your child can become so focused on what the next holiday will bring that he misses the opportunity to be a giver and not just a receiver.

The kindergarten Rite of Passage Experience enables your family to feel the power of generosity by participating in a service project together. Kindergartners learn best by experiencing life with you. Since serving others is essentially love in action, it is important for your family to do it together. If you are a single parent or even a grandparent raising a child, remember that God looks at all configurations of family as beautiful. Serving together also builds intimacy within a family unit. There is just something about ministering to others that creates closeness and a bond that are difficult to replicate. Your child can learn to embrace generosity and begin to give back—not just take—at school, at home, in the community, and with friends.

The first step in this Rite of Passage Experience is to talk with your child about the needs around him. Talk to him about what the Bible says regarding generosity and service. (If you need help, refer to the Laying the Foundation of Faith section on page 58.) Think back to your childhood. When was the first time you remember acting out of generosity? Did your family participate in service projects? Share your memories (or lack of memories) with your child, and explain why you think generosity and service are important. Ask your child to examine your own family's situation. Remember that a child this young will focus better if the discussion is simple.

We know some families who started on family service projects when their child was in kindergarten and maintained these projects throughout their child's high school years.

After your initial discussion, the next step is to ask your child to list things he sees wrong with the world. You can jot down what he says if he does not yet write. This exercise can be incredibly rewarding, because it may be the first time your child looks around to notice the pain others experience. As you review the list, ask him to choose one or two things he wants to help change for those affected. Obviously you will need to help your child think through these issues and talk about how to help in practical ways. In this powerful moment, your child will realize he has the ability to influence someone else for good.

Once the project is chosen, set a date on your family calendar and make the service day a reality. Keep it simple and have fun! Be sure to take a photo of your family during or after the service project. Frame it and display it in your child's bedroom. This photograph will serve as a tangible reminder for him to live a life of service—a symbol for unleashing generosity in his life. Your child may only be in kindergarten, but he was created to make a difference in the world around him.

This Rite of Passage Experience will shape your kindergartner's heart and teach him to live a generous life. It has the added benefit of having an impact on the rest of the family too.

Testimony:

When we set out to do our service project, our son listed twenty-seven things he wanted to do to change the world. To be honest, his list overwhelmed my wife and me. We finally helped him narrow down the list and choose just one. Our son loved his "doggie" so much from when he was a baby that he wanted to buy blankets and stuffed animals for other babies. We shopped for the baby blankets and toys, and then delivered them to the local pregnancy center.

It ended up being so simple. One mistake we made was overplanning. We wanted it to be such a grand experience that we ended up procrastinating. The lesson learned? Keep it simple! The project didn't have to be a grand experience because the service itself was so impacting.

For us, the symbol of the family picture serving together has been the most powerful part. We continually refer to the picture hanging in his room, and it helps us teach our son over and over about being generous. He's reminded of the feeling we had serving together and helping others.

A kindergartner's dad

Resource

Service project ideas

- Serve a meal at the Salvation Army.
- Collect blankets or coats to donate to a shelter or pregnancy center.
- Donate tissues or socks to elderly people in a nursing home.
- Sponsor a child through an organization such as Compassion International or World Vision.
- In lieu of birthday presents, adopt a cause and ask people to donate.

- Volunteer at a local food pantry or soup kitchen.
- Have a yard sale to benefit a particular cause (cancer research, local children's hospital, animal shelter).
- Spend time with an elderly man or woman at a nursing home.
- Hold a neighborhood food drive to donate to a food bank.
- Clean up trash in a park.
- Plant flowers at a school.
- Donate quarters to people at a Laundromat.
- Take water to a construction crew working near your home or school.
- Help an elderly person or couple in your neighborhood by pulling weeds out of their flower beds.
- Ask your child's school counselor about the biggest need in his school, and find a way to meet that need.

Laying the Foundation of Faith

One of the most important things you can do for your child at this age is to encourage an attitude of thankfulness while also cultivating sensitivity to the needs of others. God's Word provides a solid foundation for teaching this principle. The Bible is full of stories and examples of God providing for His children, so feel free to choose the passages that resonate with your family. The goal is to guide your child to consider three major questions:

1. What do I have?
2. What can I do with what I have?
3. Who around me needs help?

Let's consider an example for each one of these.

What do I have?
Matthew 14:14–21: Jesus Feeds the Five Thousand

When Jesus landed and saw a large crowd, he had compassion on them and healed their sick.

As evening approached, the disciples came to him and said, "This is a remote place, and it's already getting late. Send the crowds away, so they can go to the villages and buy themselves some food."

Jesus replied, "They do not need to go away. You give them something to eat."

"We have here only five loaves of bread and two fish," they answered.

"Bring them here to me," he said. And he directed the people to sit down on the grass. Taking the five loaves and the two fish and looking up to heaven, he gave thanks and broke the loaves. Then he gave them to the disciples, and the disciples gave them to the people. They all ate and were satisfied, and the disciples picked up twelve basketfuls of broken pieces that were left over. The number of those who ate was about five thousand men, besides women and children.

In the passage above, the disciples gave Jesus all they had—and it was enough. In fact, there were leftovers!

What can I do with what I have?
Luke 10:30–37: The Story of the Good Samaritan

> In reply Jesus said: "A man was going down from Jerusalem to Jericho, when he was attacked by robbers. They stripped him of his clothes, beat him and went away, leaving him half dead. A priest happened to be going down the same road, and when he saw the man, he passed by on the other side. So too, a Levite, when he came to the place and saw him, passed by on the other side. But a Samaritan, as he traveled, came where the man was; and when he saw him, he took pity on him. He went to him and bandaged his wounds, pouring on oil and wine. Then he put the man on his own donkey, brought him to an inn and took care of him. The next day he took out two denarii and gave them to the innkeeper. 'Look after him,' he said, 'and when I return, I will reimburse you for any extra expense you may have.'
>
> "Which of these three do you think was a neighbor to the man who fell into the hands of robbers?"
>
> The expert in the law replied, "The one who had mercy on him."
>
> Jesus told him, "Go and do likewise."

In the Bible story above, the Samaritan man showed compassion for the injured man and helped him. He used the resources and skills God had given him to serve someone else.

Who around me needs help?
Mark 2:1–12: Jesus Forgives and Heals a Paralyzed Man

A few days later, when Jesus again entered Capernaum, the people heard that he had come home. They gathered in such large numbers that there was no room left, not even outside the door, and he preached the word to them. Some men came, bringing to him a paralyzed man, carried by four of them. Since they could not get him to Jesus because of the crowd, they made an opening in the roof above Jesus by digging through it and then lowered the mat the man was lying on. When Jesus saw their faith, he said to the paralyzed man, "Son, your sins are forgiven."

Now some teachers of the law were sitting there, thinking to themselves, "Why does this fellow talk like that? He's blaspheming! Who can forgive sins but God alone?"

Immediately Jesus knew in his spirit that this was what they were thinking in their hearts, and he said to them, "Why are you thinking these things? Which is easier: to say to this paralyzed man, 'Your sins are forgiven,' or to say, 'Get up, take your mat and walk'? But I want you to know that the Son of Man has authority

on earth to forgive sins." So he said to the man, "I tell
you, get up, take your mat and go home." He got up,
took his mat and walked out in full view of them all.
This amazed everyone and they praised God, saying,
"We have never seen anything like this!"

There are people all around us in our homes, schools, and communities who need help. We just have to slow down and pray for God to show us their needs.

What You Need to Know about Kindergartners

Children in kindergarten are, in some ways, relatively self-sufficient. Physically, they have the large motor skills needed for activities such as running, jumping, and skipping, as well as the fine motor skills needed for self-care, like working buttons, zipping zippers, and tying shoes. At this age, children embrace relationships and enjoy cooperation and playtime with friends. They may also begin to ask questions about spiritual matters as they become more aware of the world and people around them.

One of the most common marks of kindergarten children is the newfound ability to think outside of themselves. As they enjoy new experiences outside of home, kindergartners suddenly become aware of the feelings of others. They learn to experience empathy. They begin to verbalize their emotions. The combination of their curious, independent nature and empathetic, teachable spirits creates the perfect time to introduce children to the practice of generosity.

Physically, kindergartners:

- Perform large motor skills (running, jumping, leaping, sliding, skipping)
- Engage in one to two minutes of sustained moderate-to-intense physical activity, leading to increased heart rate, breathing, and perspiration
- Lift and support their own body weight for a variety of activities (hopping, jumping, hanging)
- Show left- or right-handed dominance
- Perform self-care tasks with fine motor dexterity (zipping, buttoning)

Emotionally, kindergartners:

- Understand the difference between right and wrong
- Verbalize feelings appropriately
- Want to make decisions for themselves
- Are willing to take safe risks

Relationally, kindergartners:

- Enjoy playing independently or cooperatively with friends without constant supervision
- Encourage others

- Respect authority figures
- Recognize that others have feelings

Spiritually, kindergartners:

- Better understand what they see and hear (This is a great time to begin reading Bible stories to your child if you haven't already.)
- Ask questions about spirituality because of their desire to learn
- Instinctively calm themselves down and correct their own behavior due to their developing ability to manage feelings
- Have very close relationships with Mom and Dad, who have a great deal of influence at this stage

2

First Grade: An Invitation to Responsibility

First-grade teachers often tell us the changes children undergo between the time they enter first grade and when they graduate are monumental. Incrementally, students learn how to deal with more responsibility, and the expectations from parents, teachers, friends, relatives, and neighbors are greater than and different from those of previous years.

Chances are good you have already noticed changes in growth and maturity in your first grader. When a child enters first grade, she often develops a sense of confidence with this new status. Having made friends and gaining a better understanding of what to expect from teachers, first graders usually feel pretty good about the next stage of life.

What they don't know is that things are about to change again. Upon starting first grade, the demands of school and life begin to ramp up to a whole new level. People they trust most—their teachers, parents, and friends—expect more from them now than they did before. First graders may experience homework for the first time and are capable of helping with more chores around the house. They may even be invited to spend the night with a friend—away from home. In a nutshell, your child will become, in her eyes, a big kid.

First grade is possibly one of the first times your child will be given such a large amount of responsibility. We love the word *responsibility* because it's one of those words that is self-defined. Responsibility is quite simply "the ability to respond." Think of the first responders reporting to the scene of a fire or car accident. They have trained, prepared, and have the ability to respond to the crises in their communities. As adults, we also have the ability to respond to the situations we face in life. Whether it is the expectations of others, daily tasks, a crisis at work, or someone in need, we have many opportunities to respond with the love of Jesus Christ. This is a beautiful life skill to teach at this stage in your child's development.

Responsibility may not sound like an exciting character trait to celebrate, but nothing could be further from the truth. Responsibility is fundamental to so many other amazing characteristics we all want for our children. Integrity, courage, bravery, work ethic, leadership, and sensitivity to others are all built on the foundation of responsibility.

On a daily basis, strive to parent in such a way that will cause the thirty-five-year-old version of your child to say, "Thank you." Teaching her responsibility at such a young age will give her a much better chance at becoming a responsible adult.

Before you begin to panic about how fast time is moving, remember that guiding your kid into adulthood is a major part of your job description. Instead of dreading the increased burdens of the first grade year, embrace them as an opportunity to teach your child how to respond to various demands on her time and attention. Rather than just moving up another year in school, welcome your child to "big kid" status with some special moments and experiences. Every first grader wants to be a big kid, so embrace the opportunity.

First Grade Rite of Passage
Ceremony: Presentation of Blessing Box
Symbol: Blessing Box and letters

The first grade Rite of Passage Experience centers on a special item called the Blessing Box. It is literally a box filled with letters from important people in your child's life. Don't get caught up in the actual box—it can be a shoe box covered in wrapping paper, a decorated plastic box, or a specially purchased treasure box. We've even known some parents who have turned the box into a major art project they worked on with their child. Regardless, the box itself is only significant because of what it contains.

To prepare the contents of your child's Blessing Box, choose a person who represents each area of responsibility (school, family, church, and friendship). It can be a teacher, sibling, grandparent, and pastor, for example. Ask each person to write a letter to your child, specifically outlining how he or she has seen your child being responsible and encouraging her to continue on that path. Write a letter to your child as well, and include specific examples of responsible actions. Please understand, this is *not* a time to correct your child or to spur improvement in certain areas. The goal is to put wind in your child's sails, not take it out and steer her off course.

Once you have collected the letters from everyone participating in this rite of passage, place the letters inside the Blessing Box and designate a special time to present it to her. (If you need ideas for the letters or how to present them, check out the sample letters on page 69 and 70.)

When you are ready to present the Blessing Box, set aside a time when there won't be other distractions. Read the letters with her. Remind her of the areas she has shown responsibility, emphasize how proud you are of her choices, and congratulate her on becoming a big kid. Stay focused on the areas in which she is responsible, and resist the temptation to mention any areas where she is struggling to be responsible. That is a conversation for another time. Make sure to pray with her, and ask God to help her continue to be responsible as she grows up by choosing to do what is right.

Keep in mind that children in first grade take huge steps in their levels of responsibility. For some children, it can be challenging and even overwhelming. Over the course of the year, you will probably witness some meltdowns and feelings of inadequacy or insecurity. However, remember that each challenging moment is an opportunity to infuse faith in your child's life. Continue to point her toward God and His Word, shower her with encouragement, remind her to read her Blessing Box letters, and cover her with prayer. First grade is a fun year—make the most of it as you continue this amazing journey to pass on faith.

Resources

Sample invitation to friends and family to participate

Dear _____,

_____ (insert child's name) is in first grade this year, so we want to encourage him/her in the area of responsibility and integrity. Since you play an important role in his/her life, would you take a moment to write a short letter? It would mean a lot to him/her and to our family.

We are going to put the letters in a special Blessing Box and give them to him/her in a few weeks. I have included a sample letter to help you, in case you need ideas. Thank you for your time and your investment in _____ (insert child's name).

Sample responsibility letter to child from teacher/coach/friend

Dear _____,

I am so thankful for the opportunity to be your _____ (teacher/coach/friend). You are really growing up! Over the past months/weeks/years, I have noticed that you are becoming very responsible.

You choose to _____ and help _____ with _____.

I have noticed you _____during school/practice/church.

All these things show you are a young person of integrity. Integrity means you are truthful with your words and actions, no matter who is watching.

I am so proud of you and the choices you are making. I love being your _____ (teacher/coach/friend).

Sample responsibility letter to child from parent

Dear _____,

I am so proud of the big kid you are becoming. At home/at school/in friendship with _____, you have been _____.

You take such good care of _____, and you remember to _____.

I have noticed your willingness to help with _____.

I see you choosing to do what is right when you _____.

All these things show you are responsible.

I love watching you become the big girl/boy God created you to be. I am so thankful that God gave you to me. You have shown me that you can be a big kid who is responsible. I am so proud of you for allowing God to shape who you are. It's good to be your mom/dad/parents.

Blessing Box presentation script

We've been talking a lot about all the responsibilities you have at school, at home, and with your friends. Responsibility means taking good care of the things under your control. While learning about responsibility, you have shown us that you are a big kid and are ready to do your best in all of these areas. We asked your _____
(teacher/uncle/piano teacher) to write letters to you about the responsible behaviors they've seen in you. We've placed them inside this Blessing Box, and we want to read them to you.

(Read the letters, saving the letter from you for last.)

This is your Blessing Box. You can take the letters out at any time and read them to remember what we think of you. We are so proud of how responsible you've been at home, with your friends, and at school. You are ready to be a big kid. As you get older, the amount of responsibility will grow—just like you will grow. When that time comes, I know you will be ready because you are learning to trust God and be responsible now.

We are so blessed to have you as our son/daughter. We love you. Welcome to the world of being a big kid!

Testimony:

We asked special people in Brandon's life to write a letter of blessing to him. We were thrilled that every person we asked was excited about writing the letter. They ended up being much more creative than my husband or I were with our letters.

Around Brandon's birthday in April, we had a barbecue at the house. Each person who wrote a letter was invited, along with some other friends and family. We sat around our picnic table and read the letters of blessing to Brandon. Grandma and Grandpa teared up. We laughed, cried, and when we were finished, my husband and I prayed a prayer of blessing over little Brandon.

During the entire ceremony, his eyes were as big as saucers with excitement. When we finished praying, Brandon said, "Can we do that again next year?" The experience was extra special for Brandon and all of us as well.

A first grader's mom

Laying the Foundation of Faith

Why is responsibility an important quality to encourage in your child's development? It is the outward result of an internal sense of right and wrong. A responsible child is more likely to develop a strong work ethic, express sensitivity to others, exhibit leadership qualities, and operate as a person of integrity. The world desperately needs more people of integrity who take responsibility for their choices and stand up for what is right.

If God said you could have anything you wanted, what would you ask of Him? In the Bible, God asked King Solomon this question, and Solomon's answer was "wisdom." Wisdom is the ability to know what is true and right. Responsibility is the capacity to follow through and actually do it. Rooted in integrity and a sense of duty, responsibility enables your child to turn spiritual truths (wisdom) into actionable steps.

The Bible has a vast amount to say about these truths, so spend some time reading and studying. Here are a few verses to get you started:

> Choose my instruction instead of silver, knowledge
> rather than choice gold. (Prov. 8:10)

> The tongue of the wise adorns knowledge, but the
> mouth of the fool gushes folly. (Prov. 15:2)

> Whoever can be trusted with very little can also be
> trusted with much. (Luke 16:10)

A friend loves at all times. (Prov. 17:17)

Whatever you do, work at it with all your heart.
(Col. 3:23)

As you can see, the Bible is packed with encouragement for being responsible. Since there are so many chances during first grade for you to teach and show responsibility, there are an equal number of chances to infuse faith into your child's life. Becoming a big kid is an exciting prospect for children, so there is no end to the ways you can reinforce, inspire, and foster responsibility in the life of your child.

Most children at this age engage with the world in four primary settings: home, school, lessons and practices (dance, piano, violin, soccer, hockey, and so on), and situations with friends.

At home, your first grader is ready to assume more responsibility, although she may not always want to do so. She can unload a dishwasher, put clean clothes away, make her bed, and organize her toys. Your child may even be mature enough to feed your family's pet or pets. Asking her to participate in your household by helping with chores encourages independence, a sense of accomplishment, and the value of cooperation.

School—whether traditional or homeschool—provides unlimited opportunities to teach your child about responsibility. From organizing her backpack and remembering homework assignments to helping her teacher with classroom chores and being a good line leader, your child can see the results of making responsible choices every day.

Cooperation is also an essential skill in friendship. More than likely, your child can name several people she considers friends. First grade is a great time to help your child learn that having friends also means being a good friend. Ways to be responsible in friendship are keeping promises, playing fair, taking turns, and asking for and offering forgiveness.

What You Need to Know about First Graders

As you have probably observed, most first graders tend to be in perpetual motion. They enjoy games of chase or tag and look for ways to test their muscle strength (throwing, kicking, catching). Their schoolwork can be sloppy, but it may be because some kids do things in such a hurry or because they're working on their dexterity. They still tend to be a little egocentric and oversensitive, but they are also more aware of their emotions and those of others. At this age, rules and repetition provide security, so it is an ideal time to introduce or increase chores and invite them to understand their roles in the household.

Physically, first graders:

- Tend to be in constant motion: squirm, gesture while talking, and so on
- Test muscle strength by skipping, running, throwing, catching
- May be sloppy because they tend to do things in a rush

- Can tire easily because of the fast pace at which they do things
- Engage in a lot of chasing games, specifically boy/girl chasing on the playground

Emotionally, first graders:

- Begin to distinguish reality from fantasy
- Play more dramatically
- Can't fully process a consequence before they execute an action
- Tend to be oversensitive and even moody
- Have a tendency to still be egocentric
- Move more toward independence and spend a good deal of time apart from family
- Are more aware of their own emotions and those of others
- See things as black and white, with no middle ground

Relationally, first graders:

- Tattle on others
- Need rules and rituals
- Seek opportunities for unmonitored social interactions
- Care what others think about them
- Begin asking for privacy

- Focus on friendships with peers
- Play with friends of the same gender
- Have a few close friends they play with more than others

Spiritually, first graders:

- Begin asking questions, some possibly difficult to answer, that may make you squirm (It might be a good time to admit you don't always have the answers.)
- Develop a sense of morality, seeing things as right or wrong through the lens of parents and teachers and tending to have strong convictions of right and wrong
- See themselves as the center of the universe and are proud of their accomplishments, therefore needing help learning the difference between confidence and boasting
- Are just beginning to think of others

3

Second Grade: An Invitation to the Bible

When a child enters second grade, he will begin spending a lot more time reading because one of the educational goals in most second-grade curricula is for students to become independent readers who master this critical skill. Whether your child is struggling to read with fluency or is already an avid bookworm at the beginning of second grade, he is almost guaranteed to be a better reader by the end of the school year.

Because your child is learning how to be an independent reader, it is a great time to invite him to engage with the Bible in a new way. As an adult, you know how hard it can be to make time for personal Bible reading, but the second-grade emphasis on reading provides an amazing opportunity to tie your child's need to read with a need for faith—and help him form a lifelong habit of reading God's Word. As your child gets to know characters in the various books he reads, introduce him to the real people and true stories in the Bible. As he practices retelling and writing his own stories, you can point him to the ultimate story of life and faith in the Bible.

There is no way your second grader will understand everything in the Bible. We both have educational degrees in ministry and yet, like you, we still have much to learn from God's Word. Consider the fact that because your child is now reading independently, this may be the first time he will read the Bible by himself. As such, this is the perfect age to incorporate the rite of passage of giving your child a special Bible. It's also a great time to help him understand what the psalmist meant when he said, "Your word is a lamp for my feet, a light on my path" (Ps. 119:105).

At this age, your child depends on you to instruct him in the ways of faith, yet he is moving toward practicing the Christian faith on his own. Through our studies in faith development, we have learned that kids first live out the faith of their family and eventually acquire a more mature belief system they personally own. Reading the Bible on a regular basis—even as a second grader—can help your child form one of the most important, positive habits of his life. Second grade is an excellent time to reinforce simple Bible concepts, such as "God loves you unconditionally," and help your young person develop a short but consistent time of reading the Word of God.

Second Grade Rite of Passage
Ceremony: Bible presentation
with Scripture testimony
Symbol: Bible

In the second grade Rite of Passage Experience, you and others who are important to your child will have the chance to share why the Bible is meaningful to you, and then you will present your child with his very own Bible. As a parent, your treatment of Scripture greatly forms how your child will treat Scripture, so this experience is a wonderful gateway to influence him concerning the power and impact of God's Word.

The first step is to purchase a Bible. This Bible will serve as a tangible reminder of everything you are impressing on your child's heart over the course of this year, so choose one that is age appropriate and easy for him to understand. Today's bookstores and online retailers sell Bibles in a variety of translations, with decorative covers, creative clasps, and even tabs to easily find all the books. You may even want to have your child's name engraved on the cover.

After you purchase the Bible, ask significant people in your child's life to highlight their favorite verses and write their names or initials next to those verses. We also recommend that you write a short letter to your child in the front of the Bible. (See the sample letter in the resource section.)

Once the Bible is ready, present it to your child. Take time to read the letter inside the cover and point out some of the verses people highlighted. By presenting your child with his Bible, you are also giving him an invitation to experience God's Word independently and be a part of God's story. Storytelling is powerful, and the stories found in the Bible are life changing! You have the ability to make an eternal difference in the life of your child by intentionally introducing him to the Bible. How exciting to watch him pick up this great book and then read it—all on his own.

When my (Jim's) daughter was about four years old, I found her sitting in the chair that my wife, Cathy, always sat in to do her daily Bible reading and devotions. Heidi was holding a *Star*

Wars magazine upside down, turning the pages. I asked her what she was doing. "Votions," she replied, as she imitated Cathy's daily discipline. Even as she got older, Heidi realized, since her parents took time to read the Bible daily and pray, maybe she should also. When it comes to the discipline of Bible reading, more is caught than taught.

Testimony:

We decided to do our second grader's Rite of Passage Experience right after Christmas. My husband and I went to the bookstore and waded through all the Bibles until we found one with a lion on the front that looked really cool. It was also the translation we wanted our son to have because it was easy to read and understand. Over the holidays, we passed the Bible around to family and friends and let them mark their favorite verses and then write a short note in the front of the Bible.

When the night came to present the Bible, it truly felt a bit like Christmas morning because I was so excited. We started with a special family dinner in which we each took some time to talk about what the Bible means to us. After dinner, we brought out the Bible. We had decided not to wrap it, because when our son sees wrapping paper, he immediately thinks it's a toy. We wanted him to see this differently. We handed him the Bible and explained to him what all the notes and markings inside of it meant. I have to confess I was a bit disappointed. I was hoping for a lot of excitement, but my son was quiet and thoughtful. He thanked us, and that was it.

Later that night, I noticed my son had gone to bed a little earlier to do his nightly reading. (He reads books for school every night.) When I passed his room, I looked in and saw that he was not reading library

books from school. He was furiously flipping through his new Bible looking up the favorite verses that friends and family members had marked.
My son was excited to read his Bible! It remains one of the most special
gifts we have ever given him.

A second grader's mom

Resource

Sample letter from parent to child

Dear _____,

   *As a second grader, you have developed into an amazing reader. We
want you to learn to love the greatest book of all time: the Bible. Some of
the people who love you most have taken the time to mark their favorite
verses in this Bible. We hope it will be a guide for you as you seek to know
God on your own.*

Love, Mom and Dad

Date: _____

Laying the Foundation of Faith

This year, you have the opportunity to teach your child that the Bible
is not just a book to take to church but a personal, true story that
will fuel his faith and friendship with God. You have the chance
to impress upon your child the wonder and mystery of the greatest
story ever told. God desires for *you* to be one of the first people to
introduce your child to His amazing story as told through the pages

of the Bible. You get to experience the joy of sharing and reading God's story together.

Because it is so vital for your child to know and love God's Word, it's important to make sure you don't give him a negative impression of the Bible. Contrary to what some believe (or model), the Bible is not

- a rule book,
- a task to be checked off a list,
- a behavior-modification tool, or
- a self-help book.

The Bible is so much more! It is a personal letter from God that tells His story of love and redemption. God has breathed life into Scripture. Reading the Word of God orients your child to a biblical worldview that has eternal value. It teaches what is true. It can make people's lives whole again. It trains us to do what is right and helps correct our mistakes. The Bible is a source of comfort, knowledge, inspiration, and power. By reading and absorbing Scripture, a child of God will be prepared to do "every good thing" (see 2 Tim. 3:16–17), including interacting well with others, committing to purity, leading others, handling money responsibly, and living with integrity.

Basically this rite of passage gives your child the understanding written in Isaiah 40:8: "The grass withers and the flowers fall, but the word of our God endures forever."

The majority of families today live overcrowded lifestyles. At times we become overcommitted with our schedules and underconnected with our primary relationships. We also find it difficult to consistently have our own personal devotion time with God. But this year can be different: begin to read a portion of Scripture with your child on a regular basis—whether it's a whole Bible story or just a few verses, the important thing is consistency.

Psychologists tell us it takes about three weeks to create a habit. Why not focus a few minutes each day with your child on placing the Word of God in your hearts and minds? It can be during a meal or at bedtime or even on the drive to school. This habit will be life transforming for your child and for you.

Don't expect every moment spent reading the Bible or praying with your child to be a huge spiritual event. It is more about the faithfulness of regularly putting the Word of God into your minds and hearts and the long-term fruit that grows as a result.

For many years I (Jim) tried to pray with my kids individually each night. For some reason I got in the habit of drawing the sign of the cross on their foreheads with my finger. I really don't remember ever having a conversation about that ritual; we just did it.

My daughter Christy went away to college and then lived away from our home in another city after graduation. About five years later, circumstances in her life brought her back home for a time. It was a very tough season for her. One evening I walked into her room where she was in bed, reading. It had been a particularly difficult day for her, so I asked her if I could pray. She said yes. I sat down on the edge of her bed and prayed. When I moved to leave, she grabbed my hand and drew the sign of the cross on her forehead with my finger. She didn't see the tears in my eyes as I kissed her on the forehead and walked out of her room. Until that moment I had no idea that ritual was ever important to her.

> But as for you, continue in what you have learned and have become convinced of, because you know those from whom you learned it, and how from infancy you have known the Holy Scriptures, which are able to make you wise for salvation through faith in Christ Jesus. All Scripture is God-breathed and is useful for teaching, rebuking, correcting and training in righteousness, so that the servant of God may be thoroughly equipped for every good work. (2 Tim. 3:14–17)

> This is the disciple who testifies to these things and who wrote them down. We know that his testimony is true.
> Jesus did many other things as well. If every one of them were written down, I suppose that even the whole world would not have room for the books that would be written. (John 21:24–25)

> Your word is a lamp for my feet,
>   a light on my path. (Ps. 119:105)

> "All people are like grass,
>   and all their faithfulness is like the flowers of
>   the field...."

The grass withers and the flowers fall,
>   but the word of our God endures forever.
>   (Isa. 40:6, 8)

Tell your child about your favorite Bible story. Even better, let him read it to you! Use his newfound skill of reading to connect him to God and begin to build a foundation of faith in your home.

What You Need to Know about Second Graders

Physical growth patterns vary widely in second graders, resulting in vast differences in size and physical abilities among groups of children. Emotionally, children begin to reason logically and become sensitive to adult evaluations—hence the need for encouraging parents, grandparents, teachers, and leaders. One of the biggest developmental jumps in the life of a second grader is in the area of social skills. Kids begin to develop meaningful friendships, find security and significance in groups or teams, and recognize the needs and feelings of others.

As we mentioned earlier in the chapter, another big milestone is reading independently. Not only does this have an impact on your child academically, but it also builds confidence and independence in every area of his life. Just think! Your child can read a menu and order a meal at restaurants, follow simple instructions to build a new toy, and help prepare a meal or treat by reading a recipe. More important, reading enables your child to explore the Bible on his own.

Physically, second graders:

- Might have vast differences in size and physical abilities compared to other second graders, which may affect self-image
- May not want to rest when tired
- Should be riding a two-wheel bicycle without training wheels
- Can take on more responsibility around the home, such as vacuuming and helping look after younger siblings
- Have well-developed hand-eye coordination

Emotionally, second graders:

- Are sensitive to adult evaluation
- Care very much about fairness
- Become more serious
- Begin to reason logically
- Want to assume more responsibility
- Have rising levels of confidence in school

Relationally, second graders:

- Compare themselves to others, which can lead to self-criticism
- Place importance on friendships

- Seek security in groups, clubs, sports teams, and so on
- Begin to understand others' perspectives

Spiritually, second graders:

- See things as right or wrong, black or white, with no middle ground
- Begin to recognize differences in others' beliefs and may have questions as to why other children believe differently
- Can understand reasoning and make right decisions
- Have a tendency to worry more than in the past
- Need encouragement from parents, particularly because self-comparison to peers is high

4

Third Grade: An Invitation to Rhythm

The rhythm rite of passage is a unique one; it sort of sneaks up on parents and kids. When we did a focus group with parents of third graders, we were surprised by the intensity and number of comments about parents' new roles as taxi drivers and keepers of the schedule. They talked a lot about their children's involvement in activities such as sports, dance, gymnastics, music lessons, birthday parties, family events, and a larger homework load. These parents were overwhelmed by "busyness." One mom told us, "Our schedule is so complicated we use a computer printout to make sure we cover all the things we are involved in."

Our invitation to rhythm in this rite of passage is not about musical rhythm but rather time and the rhythm of life. At this stage in your child's life, you can quickly send the family schedule into chaos if you're not careful. Many third graders are developing new interests and talents. They want to be involved in everything, and sometimes parents are guilty of keeping the calendar overcrowded because the opportunities for their children are almost unlimited.

This is the year to teach your child (and maybe yourself) about making wise choices with her priorities, as well as finding a healthy rhythm for her life. While this lesson begins in third grade, we've no doubt it will continue for a lifetime. Making good decisions about rhythms of life, rest, priorities, and stewardship of time is as significant to character development as anything else.

Third Grade Rite of Passage
Ceremony: Presentation of rhythm symbol
Symbol: Timepiece (watch, hourglass, calendar, planner, clock)

The third grade Rite of Passage Experience ties together all the elements important to developing a healthy rhythm to life. One of the definitions of *rhythm* is "movement, fluctuation, or variation marked by the regular recurrence or natural flow of related elements."[1] Rhythm in your daily schedule means allowing all the activities and events in your life to flow together naturally. It means your family calendar should come together in a harmonious and pleasing blend, rather than a disorganized, chaotic cacophony. Does it sound impossible? It doesn't have to be. There will always be times when your family schedule gets out of whack, but the goal is greater balance, not perfection.

The truth is, God has given every person an equal amount of time in a day. He has also given each person individual gifts, interests, and needs. Learning to prioritize and manage time to maximize the gifts God has given you is an important skill that will benefit you and your children for the rest of your lives.

Beginning in third grade, kids are pulled in different directions. They need to learn how to make the most of every moment they have. By teaching your child to manage a schedule and set priorities, you will also help her see the importance of rest and spending time with God. Since children are concrete thinkers, it is important to give your child a tangible representation of this year's emphasis on rhythm.

To prepare for the Rite of Passage Experience, choose a gift for your child that commemorates the commitment to rhythm in your family. You can choose a new watch, an hourglass, a themed calendar, an appealing planner, or even a family heirloom timepiece or clock. It all depends on what you think your child would like and what works best for your family.

Once you have the gift, present it to your child during a special time, possibly at the dinner table or at a designated rite of passage occasion. If the gift is a family heirloom, consider enlisting a family member to share a story about it. No matter what type of gift you choose, make sure to affirm your child in her search for a healthy rhythm and pray together to ask God for wisdom to maintain balance in her life. (A sample script is provided later as a resource.) A big part of this rite of passage is to spend some time teaching your third grader the power of prioritizing time, including the scriptural mandate for rest (Sabbath).

When God said we should have a regular rhythm of rest, it was a command, not a suggestion. That is because God made us and, as a part of His design, He wanted us to stop and commune with Him. The Sabbath rest is a gift from God. He promises us that if we choose to trust Him and honor the Sabbath, He will multiply our work.

One of our favorite examples of this is when Truett Cathy, the founder of Chick-fil-A, decided that his restaurant would be closed on Sundays to honor the Sabbath—despite the potential earnings he would lose. God honored Truett's obedience, and Chick-fil-A is now one of the most successful fast-food restaurants in the nation.

Another part of the rhythm discussion with your third grader should be about the difference between physical rest and spiritual rest. When God calls us to honor the Sabbath, He is not telling us to spend the day taking naps and playing video games. Although physical rest is part of the Sabbath, the main purpose is to spend time building our relationships with God. What a great truth to pass on to your child and yourself!

Resource

Sample script for rhythm presentation

As you grow older and your life involves more events, experiences, and time, we want to encourage you to take a look at your rhythm of priorities, especially concerning your time with God and at rest. Having a good rhythm of priorities means it is okay to say no to some things in order to say yes to things that are most important. We want to help you figure out a plan to enjoy the activities you love most, spend time with God, and get the rest you need each week. To create this plan, we will list the activities that are currently in your weekly schedule and evaluate if they match your priorities. We'll also decide which activities we might be able to live without so there is margin in our schedule to grow in our relationship with God and with each other as a family. We believe you are ready to take on this rhythm we've discussed and honor God with how you spend your time. We want to give you a _____ as a reminder to have rhythm in your life. Every time you look at it, we hope you'll remember that time is a gift from God. We all get to choose how we spend it, so ask God to help you use it well.

We love you.

Testimony:

My husband and I judge the success of our family's rhythm by how often we gather around the table for dinner. Recently, we gave in and allowed both our boys to play sports. This was fun at first, until they both had practices and games on the same night. We went from eating dinner around the table to being on a first-name basis with the teenager in the drive-through at the fast-food place by our house. It was not pretty. So we finally had to stop the madness.

We told our sons that for the next season there would be fewer sports. My first-grade son was actually thankful. He wanted a break. There was much screaming and gnashing of teeth from my third-grade boy. He didn't want to miss out. That's why I was so thankful to realize that the rite of passage for this year was the one on rhythm. When we talked to our son about the Sabbath and presented him with his first watch, we were able to talk through the decision to take basketball off our schedule.

Let's just say that we are eating a lot more dinners around the table now because my son understands why it's so important.

A third grader's mom

Laying the Foundation of Faith

When you look at your child's weekly schedule, it's probably hard
to imagine how to help her understand rhythm. Let's face it, even
parents find it difficult to maintain balance. It's important to realize
that finding a balanced rhythm in life is a *tension to manage* and not
a problem to solve. Let's take a few minutes and learn what the Bible
has to say about priorities, God time, and rest.

This Rite of Passage Experience is a great time to help your
child determine her priorities. Start by listing all the activities in
which she participates and would like to participate. Are there
natural conflicts? Are there activities that interfere with family
events or priorities? Are there activities you need to say no to in
order to focus more on other things? Are there items you need to
pray about in order to determine if they are God's best for your
child? Working together through the choices and opportunities
is a great way to teach your child how to develop her own life's
rhythm.

Conversations with your child about rhythm

Rhythm with Priorities

There is a great story in the Bible about a man named Nehemiah
who knew how to set priorities. Nehemiah was a civil servant who
worked for King Artaxerxes. His hometown of Jerusalem had been
destroyed, and he felt God calling him to return there to rebuild the
broken walls. The king granted Nehemiah permission to tackle the

vision God had given him, but the job proved very difficult. Read Nehemiah 6:1–4.

> When word came to Sanballat, Tobiah, Geshem the Arab and the rest of our enemies that I had rebuilt the wall and not a gap was left in it—though up to that time I had not set the doors in the gates—Sanballat and Geshem sent me this message: "Come, let us meet together in one of the villages on the plain of Ono."
>
> But they were scheming to harm me; so I sent messengers to them with this reply: "I am carrying on a great project and cannot go down. Why should the work stop while I leave it and go down to you?" Four times they sent me the same message, and each time I gave them the same answer.

Wow! Did you notice what Nehemiah had to do? He said no to some things in order to stay focused on his priority. In the passage above, he said no to the same meeting four different times. If you read the entire story of Nehemiah, you'll see that he constantly faced opposition and distraction during this project—even from people who were trying to "help." Nehemiah was passionate about rebuilding the walls, but he had to continually state and stick to his priorities in order to complete the project.

The same is true in your life and the life of your child. Anything important to you can be considered a priority. Your third grader has probably been presented with many opportunities in which she can engage. As a parent, you can help her understand that developing a rhythm to her life means saying yes to some things and no to others. Not everyone may agree with your choices, but the ability to say no to something is critical to having a healthy, balanced life. Being able to look at a calendar and give priority to the best things—even over the good things—will allow your child to control her schedule instead of the schedule (or other people) controlling her.

Rhythm with God Time

One of the biggest problems with having an overpacked calendar is that all the other things in life interfere with spending time with God. Third grade is the ideal age to help your child figure out a rhythm for God time—when, where, and how she'll spend time with God.

Why do we need to have consistent time with God? It is the only way to cultivate a relationship with Him. Even Jesus made sure to carve out time to talk to God. Read Mark 1:35.

> Very early in the morning, while it was still dark,
> Jesus got up, left the house and went off to a soli-
> tary place, where he prayed.

By helping your child choose and honor time with God, even if it's only for a few minutes each day, you are communicating to her the importance of developing a relationship with God.

Help your child determine the best time of day to read her Bible and pray. Is it in the morning before school, as soon as she gets home from school, after dinner, or before bed? You may initially want to be a part of her daily spiritual discipline until the habit is developed, to help her move from dependence toward greater independence.

It's also a good idea to give her a reading plan or devotion book. Maybe she can start with a few verses a day from the Bible or one lesson each day from a devotional. Whatever you and your child agree to do, have God time with her for at least the first week. Start by praying out loud together, starting with you and then allowing your child to lead. You are a model for her of how to have regular time with God.

Once your child understands the process, let her continue the God time on her own. Remember to check in with her regularly, and if she misses a day, be transparent about your own struggles to consistently spend time with God, and encourage her to keep going. This will be an ongoing conversation with your child and will allow you to infuse faith conversations into your daily life. You can ask her to share what she is learning and offer to answer any questions she has.

Rhythm with Rest

With life's craziness, another thing that can get overlooked is rest. We were made for much more than a constant cycle of work and entertainment. In fact, God commands us to create space for rest. Take a look at Genesis 2:2–3.

By the seventh day God had finished the work he
had been doing; so on the seventh day he rested
from all his work. Then God blessed the seventh
day and made it holy, because on it he rested from
all the work of creating that he had done.

God gave His absolute best, and then He rested. Rest is not
just for sleeping; it is also an opportunity to reflect, unplug, relax,
meditate, and evaluate. These are activities that don't just give us an
escape for our minds; they replenish our souls. What type of activities are we suggesting? Well, that will be different for each person.
True recreation is when you choose your own activity, and that activity leaves you feeling fully refreshed. It is a chance to connect with
God, family, and yourself. Take time to review your family calendar
and help your child understand her need for rest. Encourage her
to set aside time for rest and protect it as a priority, as with school,
homework, God time, and activities.

There might be times when you wonder how you ever made it to
the end of the day. Have you ever stopped to wonder what your child
is feeling on those days? Do you find yourself having to constantly
push her to keep up? The goal of this year is to minimize—and even
eliminate—those kinds of days.

Just think! You have the chance to lead your child on a journey
to navigate and prioritize her schedule. More than likely, no one
helped you do this until much later in life—if ever. What an amazing
thing it would be to impart God's wisdom regarding this subject and
set your child on a path to healthy rhythm. That is definitely a key
component to leaving a legacy of faith.

What You Need to Know about Third Graders

During the third-grade year, children begin to see clear differences between themselves and others. They may even begin to define themselves based on their attributes and achievements. As a result, they are more sensitive to external stressors such as homework, schedules, and expectations. They also become less dependent on parents and more dependent on peers. All of these developments can cause children to suppress their individuality in an effort to fit in. That's why this year it is appropriate and necessary to teach your child the value of rhythm in her life and schedule.

Physically, third graders:

- Grow permanent teeth
- Participate in team sports
- Recognize the broad differences in size and ability among themselves and their peers
- Have increased coordination as well as motor and stationary movement
- Have longer attention spans

Emotionally, third graders:

- Define themselves based on attributes or achievements
- Push their limits

- Have a strong desire to do things well
- Struggle to handle failure and criticism
- May become stressed because of schoolwork
- Bite off more than they can chew by overshooting abilities

Relationally, third graders:

- Place high importance on friendships and have very close friends
- Become less dependent on parents and more dependent on peers
- Begin to care for and play with younger children
- Recognize when someone is being left out and take the initiative to include him or her

Spiritually, third graders:

- Move out of the egocentric stage and begin considering others
- Begin to distinguish what is important and what is not
- Can ask important spiritual questions and tend to have significant ideas of their own
- Can rank themselves and others based on material possessions

5

Fourth Grade: An Invitation to Friendship

Think back to when you were in elementary school. Can you remember your best friends from those years? Do the memories bring a smile to your face or sadness to your heart? Either way, your friends left an impression that you can probably still recall today. There's no denying that friends wield power in your life.

At age nine or ten, your child is becoming more independent, and he is probably beginning to develop a circle of friends. In fact, fourth grade is often marked by the growth and influence of friendships.

Before you begin to worry about losing your child to peer pressure at such a young age, rest assured that the biggest influence in your child's life is still you. However, the second greatest influence comes from his circle of friends. Friends shape your child's story. So how can you intentionally teach him what God-honoring friendships should look like? Imagine what could happen if you walked with him as he learned to navigate the world of healthy friendships. No doubt your life has been enhanced by life-giving friendships, and you can help your child find and nurture lasting, deep, beautiful relationships.

Fourth Grade Rite of Passage
Ceremony: Presentation of friendship artwork
Symbol: Friendship artwork

The fourth grade Rite of Passage Experience affirms the need for God-honoring friends in your child's life. You are going to create a piece of art that celebrates godly friendship and signifies who your child is as a friend. Begin by asking several of your family members and church friends, as well as your child's friends and their parents, to give you one to two words that describe your child as a friend. Collect these words, along with pictures of your child and his friends, throughout the year. Once you have assembled the collection, create a piece of art. You can do this by buying a simple, premade picture collage frame from a local store, or you can make the artwork on your own. Consider the following ideas for creating art using the words you collected:

- Paint the words on canvas.
- Etch the words in wood.
- Sketch the words on paper and frame it, or use calligraphy or graffiti art.
- Use a collage frame to include pictures of your child's friends, along with the words those friends used to describe your child.
- Decorate a poster board with the words and photos.

There are unlimited options for making artwork that will be special to your child. Don't put pressure on yourself to create a masterpiece; the meaning and significance behind the artwork will be what's special.

Once your gift is prepared, designate a time to give it to your child. Be sure to affirm your child in the area of friendship. Name specific examples that illustrate how he is a good friend. Integrate Bible lessons about friendship. (See Laying the Foundation of Faith on page 104 for ideas.) Help him realize that the artwork is a constant reminder of the importance of being a good and kind friend. If you need some extra help planning, use the sample presentation script in the Resource section.

Resource

Sample friendship artwork presentation script

You are such a great friend. Over the past few weeks, we talked about the characteristics of a godly friend. We've learned about showing loyalty and respect, as well as the importance of being an encourager. I was proud of you when you did _____ for _____. Last week, you did _____ for _____ and that showed_____.

I asked your friends and some family members to give me a couple of words that describe you, and we used them to create a piece of art for your room. This is what your friends say you are:

(Read the words to your child.)

These words are so special because they show how you have been a good friend in our home, in our church, and in your school. Every time you see it, I want you to remember what your friends think of you and remember the kind of friend God wants you to be. We are so proud of you. We love you.

Testimony:

This is the year our daughter Rachel blossomed with her friendships. She has been so busy with birthday parties, soccer practice, and even some sleepovers with church friends. We took the scriptures from the Pass It On Experience and started talking about them during a couple of dinners.

One night we brought out the poster board that our older daughter had created just for the occasion. We asked relatives, special friends of our family, our children's director at church, and even a couple of Rachel's girlfriends to give us two words that best describe the type of person Rachel is to her family and friends. Our older daughter is very artistic, and she created a poster that read: "A Friend Loves at All Times ..." Proverbs 17:17 in the center. All around the scripture she printed words like *patient*, *fun*, *caring*, and all the other words that described our Rachel. She also put the names of the people who wrote the words.

Today, Rachel has her poster hanging in her bedroom. It was a very cool experience for Rachel and for all of us.

A fourth grader's mom

Laying the Foundation of Faith

From stories of good friends to wisdom on how to be a friend, God's Word is the ultimate resource for learning about friendship. The

Bible outlines three major characteristics of a godly friend: loyalty, respect, and encouragement.

The story of David and Jonathan is perhaps the most famous Bible story for learning about friendship. Take a moment to read 1 Samuel 18:1–4.

> After David had finished talking with Saul, Jonathan became one in spirit with David, and he loved him as himself. From that day Saul kept David with him and did not let him return home to his family. And Jonathan made a covenant with David because he loved him as himself. Jonathan took off the robe he was wearing and gave it to David, along with his tunic, and even his sword, his bow and his belt.

As you can tell from this passage, David and Jonathan were extremely close. The Bible tells us that Jonathan gave David his robe, clothes, and weapons. These items were not just some of Jonathan's favorite things. As the son of King Saul, Jonathan was a prince and a soldier. By sharing with David, he was not just giving away his material possessions, but he was also pledging his commitment, loyalty, and friendship to David.

Loyalty is the first part of a godly friendship. Help your child think about and name the friends in his life. Are there ways he can share or show his commitment and appreciation to them? Do you have a family friend with whom you could practice this concept of loyalty? Help your child think of ways to show a friend that he or she is valued and loved.

As your child begins to learn more about friendship, it is important to teach him not only what to look for in a friend, but also how to be a good friend. Consider the characteristics of a good friend. Do you have any expectations of how people should treat you and your child? Take a look at Matthew 7:12.

> So in everything, do to others what you would have them
> do to you, for this sums up the Law and the Prophets.

Respect is the second part of a godly friendship. Pause to examine your own life. Think about a time you had a disagreement with a friend or your spouse. Did you treat that person the way you want to be treated? Prayerfully list the characteristics of a godly friend, and then sit down with your child and ask him to make his own list. Show your child your list, and spend some time talking about each other's listed characteristics. Help him determine if he exhibits the characteristics of a godly friend. Remember that part of having friends is being a good friend. It is how we show respect to one another in friendship. Take time to pray with your child and ask God to help him be a godly friend.

The third part of a godly friendship is encouragement. Encouraging words lift the spirit and make a person feel strong. Words of inspiration help people believe the best and provide comfort to those who are disheartened. Teaching your child to be an encourager is like teaching him to be a bricklayer—every kind word he speaks builds someone up. Read 1 Thessalonians 5:11.

> Therefore encourage one another and build each
> other up, just as in fact you are doing.

Good friends are faithful in providing encouragement. They give support when things are tough, and they cheer on a friend who is faced with difficulty. Help your child think about the friends in his life. Spend some time talking about the special qualities of each one. Are there ways your child could provide encouragement? Take this opportunity to help him see that a good friend is one who encourages and builds up.

As you can probably attest, friends shape your life story—for better or for worse. This year, you have the chance to help your child learn to recognize and develop the characteristics of a godly friend. The goal is not just to help your child connect to good people and build strong friendships but also to discover how to be a good friend.

Since your child is maturing in his relationships, you may be surprised that his level of discussion has become more complex and thoughtful. Embrace his newfound ability and desire to connect on a mature level, and take advantage of this opportunity to enhance your relationship with him.

The teenage years are quickly approaching, so hold on a little tighter, play a little longer, and sing a little louder.

What You Need to Know about Fourth Graders

Most of the major developmental markers in fourth grade are emotional and relational. For the first time, many children form a deep relationship with a best friend. They may have secrets they share only with their friends. Many children become more emotional, exhibit worry about fitting in, or even become self-critical. Some children will even start to secretly notice the opposite sex—although they probably don't know what to do about it. Technology begins to enter the scene as some fourth graders stay in contact with their friends when they aren't at school, often through texting.

All of these elements come together to provide the perfect opportunity to process the power of friendship with your child.

Physically, fourth graders:

- Are ready for competitive and cooperative games
- Are physically maturing; some signs of puberty may appear (Girls physically mature sooner than boys.)
- May engage in habitual movements such as nail biting, hair twisting, fidgeting

Emotionally, fourth graders:

- Attempt to resolve conflict before involving adults and understand that not everyone views things the way they do
- Are no longer egocentric
- Have a high level of emotional intensity
- Can be self-critical
- May worry

Relationally, fourth graders:

- Gravitate toward certain friends
- Need encouragement
- Begin to care about social issues
- See adults as fallible, realizing their inconsistencies
- Have a strong desire to fit in
- May begin to show interest in the opposite sex
- May become deeply attached to a best friend

Spiritually, fourth graders:

- Are concerned about being right or wrong and being fair
- Experience strong inner tension between being a child and pushing toward independence
- Benefit from some freedom to exercise their growing independence
- View fairness and justice as big themes in their lives

6

Fifth Grade: An Invitation to Identity

In most schools, fifth grade is a banner year for children. In fact, your child is most likely excited to be at the top of the grade-school totem pole. This achievement is worthy of celebration, plus it's a great opportunity to help your child begin discovering her identity. Experts tell us the "primary task of the teen and preteen years is to construct a healthy sense of identity,"[1] one that will help your child become a responsible adult who loves God.

According to Merriam-Webster's online dictionary, *identity* is "the distinguishing character or personality of an individual."[2] It is essentially the qualities that make each person special and unique. God, in His infinite wisdom, made one version of your child. Before the voices of peers increase and begin to drown out your voice, you can help her fully understand and embrace the person God created her to be. Armed with a strong sense of self, your child can navigate the changing seasons of life ahead because she has roots deeply planted in the truth of God's Word.

Fifth Grade Rite of Passage
Ceremony: Affirmation of identity
Symbol: Personalized identity gift

The fifth grade Rite of Passage Experience is an opportunity to bless your child and instill confidence as she prepares to enter middle school or junior high. The experience centers on the presentation of an identity symbol that serves as a tangible reminder of the qualities that make your child unique.

Begin preparing for the gift by asking a few significant people in your child's life to write her a letter. The heart of the letters should be a description of the unique qualities or characteristics each person sees in your child. (See the sample letters later in this chapter.) Notice that we often use your child's community to speak words of affirmation, wisdom, and blessing into her life. As you think about her identity, remember that it will be shaped by her view of God, her awareness of how you view her, and what others think of her.

Once you have received the letters, review them for any consistent themes or qualities. Do most of the letters refer to the same traits (caring for others, being kind to friends, helping teachers and family)? Do certain words or phrases come up in each letter (*intelligent, funny, athletic, thoughtful, wise beyond her years*)? These references to a common characteristic can assist you in choosing an identity symbol for your child. For instance, if people say your child exhibits wisdom or intelligence, the identity symbol could be an owl. If your child invests her time, energy, and persistence into a certain sport, maybe a sports collectible or piece of sports equipment could be the symbol. Remember that you do not necessarily need to purchase an identity symbol. You may be able to make it, build it, or even engrave something that is already special to your child. The idea is to make this symbol individualized, unique, and inspirational to your child. Consider these ideas:

- Wise/intelligent: an owl or a set of books
- Athletic: sports equipment
- Kind/compassionate: a leather bracelet embossed with words/a scripture/a heart shape
- Good friend: a framed picture with friends
- Fun to be around: a piece of smiley-face jewelry, a joke book for friends/family to sign
- Creative: an art set, personalized stationery, or a camera
- Good with technology: a new device or a personalized protective case for an existing device
- Thoughtful: a journal

Set aside a time to present your child with the letters and identity symbol. Read the letters together and then explain why you chose the identity symbol you did. (See the sample Identity Symbol script to help you share the importance of this moment with your child.) Be sure to spend some time in prayer thanking God for your child and for her special attributes.

Resources

Sample letter to friend, with question guide

Dear _____,

We are preparing to celebrate the last year of elementary school* with _____. *We want to help him/her see that God made him/her special. Because you know* _____ *well, would you be willing to write a letter to celebrate the things that make him/her unique? He/she really looks up to you, and I know it would mean a lot.*

* (For most kids, fifth grade is the end of elementary school.)

It can be very short, but here are some questions you could ask in the letter:

1. *What character traits do you see in* _____?
2. *Do you notice that he/she is passionate about something in particular?*
3. *Have you noticed any special talents?*
4. *What makes him/her unique?*

Identity symbol presentation script

Over the last few weeks, I've enjoyed learning about identity with you and recognizing the ways God has made you special. We've asked a few people who know you best to write letters sharing what they see in you. Let's read those letters.

(Read the letters together.)

You can see through all these letters that one particular quality keeps coming up! It is that you are _____. While you have many other wonderful characteristics and abilities, we want you to have a symbol that will remind you that _____ is what people see in you.

(Present the symbol.)

Our prayer is that you will celebrate the things that make you unique, because those things were intentionally given to you as part of God's plan. He created you with a distinct purpose.

As you grow up, you'll continue to see these unique qualities that make you different from others. As you notice differences, celebrate the fact that God made everyone unique for a reason, and thank Him for what He wants to do in your life. Remember that He has created you to be _____.

Testimony:

At first we had a hard time figuring out what to do as a symbol for Jonathan James's Identity Rite of Passage. Then one day, I was cleaning out a box of keepsakes and saw a paper that our pastor had given us when we dedicated Jonathan James to God in a beautiful church ceremony when he was a baby. That ceremony had been meaningful to my husband and me, but of course Jonathan didn't remember it.

One of the reasons it was so special is because we were an infertile couple and had the privilege of adopting Jonathan James at birth. What a gift from God he has been in our lives. As I looked at the paper our pastor had given us on Jonathan's baby dedication day, tears welled up in my eyes. I knew this was what we should do for his symbol and ceremony for fifth grade.

We had a plaque made with these words:

Jonathan James

"God is Gracious"

"May God be gracious to you, bless you

and make His face shine upon you."

Psalm 67:1

One night after dinner we gave the plaque to Jonathan as a reminder of God's graciousness to our family for bringing our son to us.

A fifth grader's mom

Laying the Foundation of Faith

Who am I? That's a pretty big question for a kid to ask and answer—even most adults struggle with it. God created every person in His image with distinct qualities. Your goal is to help your child see herself as God sees her. How do you do that? Start by reading what He says about her in His Word.

Made for a purpose

> For you created my inmost being;
> you knit me together in my mother's womb.
> I praise you because I am fearfully and
> wonderfully made;

your works are wonderful,
     I know that full well.
My frame was not hidden from you
     when I was made in the secret place,
     when I was woven together in the depths of
          the earth.
Your eyes saw my unformed body;
     all the days ordained for me were written in
          your book
     before one of them came to be.
How precious to me are your thoughts, God!
     How vast is the sum of them!
Were I to count them,
     they would outnumber the grains of sand—
     when I awake, I am still with you.
          (Ps. 139:13–18)

This psalm contains God's thoughts about each of His children—including yours. Read these verses with your child and spend time talking and praying with her. Help her consider the following questions:

- How would you describe yourself?
- What are some things you do really well?
- What are some things you enjoy doing?
- In what areas do friends or family members ask for your help?

Keep in mind that this activity might be difficult for your fifth grader, depending on her level of comfort or desire for privacy. In fact, she may prefer to do it alone and write her answers on a piece of paper. If that's the case with your child, you may instead want to write the questions on a piece of paper for her, then allow her to answer them independently. If she is open to sharing her answers with you but too private to vocalize them, she can leave the paper in a designated area for you to review.

Whether you discuss it together or your child completes it separately, the important point to impart is that God made your child with purpose. He has a plan for her life and He wants to be involved in it.

God's bigger plan

> "For I know the plans I have for you," declares the LORD, "plans to prosper you and not to harm you, plans to give you hope and a future." (Jer. 29:11)

Encourage your child to ponder these questions:

- Do you have any big dreams?
- Have you thought about what kind of job you might want to have when you are grown?
- Are there some places you want to see or things you hope to do in your life?

If your child struggles with answering these questions, reassure her that it is okay not to know her future plans. Take the time to share some of your own dreams from childhood. It's okay if they didn't come true or if you pursued a different passion. The important thing is to help your child realize that God gives each of His children dreams and hopes, as well as the skills and talents to pursue them. By learning to seek after Him today, your child will nurture her relationship with God and allow Him to guide the choices she'll make tomorrow.

Be authentic

> When they arrived, Samuel saw Eliab and thought, "Surely the LORD's anointed stands here before the LORD."
>
> But the LORD said to Samuel, "Do not consider his appearance or his height, for I have rejected him. The LORD does not look at the things people look at. People look at the outward appearance, but the LORD looks at the heart."
>
> Then Jesse called Abinadab and had him pass in front of Samuel. But Samuel said, "The LORD has not chosen this one either." Jesse then had Shammah pass by, but Samuel said, "Nor has the LORD chosen this one." Jesse had seven of his sons pass before Samuel, but Samuel said to him, "The LORD has not chosen these." So he asked Jesse, "Are these all the sons you have?"
>
> "There is still the youngest," Jesse answered. "He is tending the sheep."

Samuel said, "Send for him; we will not sit down until he arrives."

So he sent for him and had him brought in. He was glowing with health and had a fine appearance and handsome features.

Then the LORD said, "Rise and anoint him; this is the one."

So Samuel took the horn of oil and anointed him in the presence of his brothers, and from that day on the Spirit of the LORD came powerfully upon David. Samuel then went to Ramah. (1 Sam. 16:6–13)

What does it mean to be authentic? Being authentic means being the *you* God created, not pretending to be like someone else or trying to be what you think others want you to be.

In the verses above, Samuel was given the task of anointing the next king. He knew it would be one of Jesse's sons, but he didn't know which one. When Samuel asked Jesse to line up all his sons, Jesse didn't even bring David at first!

Fortunately, God sees people differently than we do. He doesn't look at the outside appearance. In the story above, God wasn't looking for the most handsome man or the tallest son. He chose David based on the authenticity of his heart.

"Who am I?" and "Where do I fit in?" are questions your child will replay in her mind well into her teenage years. That's why inviting her to discover her identity now is critical. God made her in His image because He loves her and has a special purpose for her. By discovering these unique qualities, your child can develop a strong sense of self that is rooted in God's perfect design. A child who is confident in her identity can more easily resist temptations to give in to peer pressure or become self-critical. In fact, she may even lead others to understand and celebrate their differences as well. Everyone has an identity. This year, take the opportunity to help your child appreciate and embrace who God made her to be. Encourage your child to consider all the ways she is different and special. Pray together and thank God for the differences and plans He has in store.

What You Need to Know about Fifth Graders

Fifth graders experience an array of emotions—their moods can shift dramatically, sometimes in the same conversation. The physical and emotional development is rapid but varied at this stage, with girls usually progressing faster than boys. Kids need regular time outdoors to engage physically, but they also need times of rest (and snacks) to support all the changes in their bodies.

Relationally, ten- to eleven-year-olds become more talkative and develop humor that may not be funny to adults. As relationships with peers become more important, most children have a strong desire to fit in. Those moments are when children begin to ask, "Who am I?"

Physically, fifth graders:

- Are maturing (Girls may experience their first period.)

- Need to spend time outdoors and be challenged physically
- Benefit from snacks and rest periods, due to their rapidly growing, changing bodies
- May require reminders about good hygiene, using deodorant, brushing teeth, and so on

Emotionally, fifth graders:

- Develop their own goals
- May shrug off responsibility
- Might still be unable to manage time well and need help scheduling
- May stress over academic challenges
- Begin to accept responsibility for their failures and mistakes, though it may not be articulated

Relationally, fifth graders:

- Can independently resolve conflict and help others solve conflict
- Use humor that may not be funny to adults
- May be very talkative, especially when among friends
- Enjoy spending time with family and peers
- Often need to talk to sort through thoughts

Spiritually, fifth graders:

- Are better able to see others' perspectives and have a more global view, which facilitates empathy
- Test levels of independence (greater for boys than for girls)
- Become dependable and trustworthy
- Need help balancing time for socializing, homework, family, hobbies, sports, lessons, and so on
- Are sensitive and are able to resolve issues of fairness

7

Sixth Grade: Preparing for Adolescence

The sixth-grade year will be a season of incredibly rapid change in your child's life. In this and the coming years, most kids will experience more transformation in their development than at any other time, with the exception of the first two years of life.

You may be apprehensive about the forthcoming changes and may even be dreading the next season of parenting. (We tend to remember what we were like as adolescents!) Instead of devising a plan to banish your child (or yourself) to a room for the next few years, consider what it would look like if you intentionally and openly embraced the changes. Instead of avoiding or ignoring your child's emotional fluctuations and bodily changes, imagine what would happen if you used the changes to build a bridge toward a better relationship with your child.

This season of life is a time to influence and shape your child unlike any other. You have the privilege of helping him solidify his identity, develop confidence, and grasp the creative and amazing nature of a personal God.

Can you remember when you went through puberty? For some it was no big deal, but for many it was pretty terrible. Many parents we work with report that when they went through puberty, they were either teased or ignored by their parents. Neither is a healthy way of helping kids prepare for adolescence.

All studies show that the more kids have positive, healthy conversations with their parents about sexuality and bodily changes, the less promiscuous and confused they will be as teens. The problem is that few parents had good role models when they were growing up, and their own parents were typically silent on the matter.

It will probably feel awkward to talk to your sixth grader about the changes going on in his body, but we promise it's better than leaving him to figure it all out on his own.

Sixth Grade Rite of Passage

*Ceremony: Discussions to
prepare for adolescence
Symbol: Picture of you when
you were in sixth grade*

The goal of the sixth grade Rite of Passage Experience is to begin a habit of relationship and dialogue that will last throughout your child's teenage years. Remember, kids learn best when they talk, not when you lecture. Set aside time for conversations with your child throughout the year when he can talk about whatever is on his mind. Make active listening a major part of your relationship. Kids always view listening as a language of love.

We've helped you by developing several ten-to-fifteen-minute dialogues you can use with your child. Keep them short and simple, and try to eliminate interruptions. Focus on the changes that are coming as he enters into puberty. See Laying the Foundation of Faith on page 137 for encouragement, and use the discussion starters in the Resource section. You can choose to have just one parent or both involved in these conversations. We have found one parent sometimes works better and is less intimidating to your child, but do what works for your family.

If you can find a picture of yourself when you were in sixth grade, it is a great gift to give as a symbol for this rite of passage. We know one family who bought a three-frame picture holder and put each parent's photo and their child's sixth-grade photo in it. Much of your time together will be to share your experiences of puberty and allow him the freedom to share what's going on in his heart, mind, and body. You can refer to the photo while you are having that discussion.

By giving your child a photo of yourself at the age of eleven or twelve, he can be reminded of your conversations and remember that it is possible to survive all the changes he's going through.

When choosing time to talk with your child, pick five days that work for both of you. If you let your child help determine the days and locations for the discussions, he will take more ownership of it. Every Saturday in the kitchen, twice a week on the front porch swing, or even once a month at the park will work if you both agree to it. Many of the parents we work with tell us that just before bed tends to be a great time to get their sixth grader talking.

It is also important to eliminate outside distractions. No TV or cell phones and no other family members should be a part of your time together. Your child needs to know that you value the time you get to share with him. If at all possible, it is best if the same parent(s) or guardian participates in all five conversations. Kids generally respond better when things are consistent.

Even after you complete the five discussions, continue to set aside time to talk with your child about what is on his mind. Leverage the opportunity to talk about the things that matter most to him.

Resource

Discussion starters

Sample discussion questions are below. Feel free to write or type them, place them in envelopes marked "Parent" and "Son" (or "Daughter"), and wait to open them until you are with your child. This allows your child to feel as if he is on an even playing field. When you both open the same sealed envelopes, it feels more like you are on a journey together, and you might get more buy-in from your child. Along with the questions, there are also five devotions for you to read together. Each scheduled day, pick one question out of each envelope and ask away.

Discussion Starter #1
Parent:

When I was your age, I started noticing my body beginning to change. I needed deodorant, and there were many other differences as well. This is what you can expect too. At times I felt embarrassed about these changes, and I didn't always have someone to talk to about them. I want us to talk about these changes so you will know they are normal, and everyone goes through them.

Possible Physiological Changes for Discussion

- Acne, growth spurts, changes in voice, breast development, menstruation
- Early bloomers (body develops sooner than others) versus late bloomers (body develops later than others)
- Body hair under arms, on legs, on face (boys), and pubic hair

Questions to Ask Your Child

1. Have you noticed any of these changes with yourself or your friends?
2. How do you feel about what is happening?

Prayer

Pray that God will help your child during this time of change and will give him wisdom as he faces new feelings and changes in his life. Pray that God will give you patience and understanding to guide him through this time. Promise to listen and talk with your child about anything he is feeling. Commit to seek God's guidance through prayer and the study of Scripture.

Child:

Questions to Ask Your Parent

1. How did you feel when you were my age and went through these changes?
2. Some of my friends seem to be further along than I am and some seem to be not changing at all yet. Why is that?

Discussion Starter #2

Parent:

Very young children often say anything that comes to their minds, with no embarrassment or worry about what people think. Around the age of twelve, this begins to change. In fact, I can remember some times in my adolescence when I felt very self-conscious and felt like everyone was staring at me. I want you to know that feeling embarrassment or a heightened awareness of what others think about you is a very natural part of growing up. But I want you to know I've been there. In fact, let me tell you about one of my most embarrassing moments growing up (start the sentence with "I can remember when").

Questions to Ask Your Child

1. Do you ever wonder what people around you think about you?

2. How do you feel when you are with your friends, when you enter a classroom, and/or when you get on the bus?

3. How do you feel in youth group?

Prayer

Thank God for the blessing your child is to your family and how he is wonderfully made by God. Pray that you and your child will grow closer together and ultimately grow closer to the Lord. Ask God for wisdom to help guide your child as he begins to learn who God made him to be.

Child:

Now that I am getting older, there are some things that feel like they matter to me more than they used to—such as the clothes I wear, my hairstyle, body odor, being on time, the car we drive, some things about our family (share your thoughts about these kinds of things with your parents).

Questions to Ask Your Parent

1. Do you remember feeling different from other kids when you were my age?

2. Sometimes there are things about me and about our family that make me feel embarrassed. Did you ever feel like that when you were my age?

Discussion Starter #3

Parent:

As we change into adults, we start to become more aware of ourselves and of the people around us. This new awareness can cause us to feel a lot of different emotions, including fear, anxiety, joy, and excitement. Many kids begin to have more intense feelings during these preteen years as well. I want you to know you can always tell me how you feel about someone or any situation. I may be able to help, and I will definitely support you as you learn to cope with these new emotions.

Questions to Ask Your Child

1. Over the next few years, there are going to be times when you are moody, frustrated, or mad without really knowing why. How would you like us as a family to respond to you in those times?

2. When we disagree with each other over the next few years, what are some "rules of engagement" you think we can follow to help us deal with our conflicts?

Prayer

Read Proverbs 15:1 aloud: "A gentle answer turns away wrath, but a harsh word stirs up anger." Pray that God will impress this passage on your heart and that He will help you and your family live it out in your daily lives.

Child:

Questions to Ask Your Parent

1. When you were my age, did you ever get into arguments with your parents? If so, how did you handle it?
2. Do you think you and your parents did it the right way? How would you like us to do it differently?

Discussion Starter #4

Parent:

I'm proud that you are maturing and searching for greater understanding and answers to life's questions. There will be times when I may not have the answers, and I have to admit that, at times, I think it would be easier if you could remain a child and believe things just because I said so. But I truly want you to discover God's truth and the possibilities of a deep relationship with Him for yourself, so I am excited about your becoming a teenager.

Questions to Ask Your Child

1. Would you be willing for us to find the answers to your questions together using the Bible?
2. What advice can you give me to be the most effective parent I can be during this season of your life?

Prayer

Pray that God will give you the courage to admit when you don't know the answers to your child's questions when he comes to you. Commit to studying Scripture together to find the answers. Ask God to help you both grow in your understanding of His Word.

Child:

When I was younger, most of the time I just accepted what you and my teachers taught me to believe. Now that I'm getting older, I don't want to just take everything at face value. Sometimes I wonder if it's normal that I'm beginning to question what I've always been taught.

Questions to Ask Your Parent

1. Did you always believe the way you do now about God?
2. When and why did you change?
3. Where and how did you find answers?

Discussion Starter #5
Parent:

As you grow over these next few years, there will be a lot of changes. You are changing from being a child to becoming an adult. There are fun and exciting things about becoming an adult, and there are also difficult things about these changes. Sometimes I wish I could wrap you up and protect you from the adult world. At other times, I want to help push you forward into adulthood.

Questions to Ask Your Child

1. Do you feel nervous or afraid about anything you see happening with yourself or your friends?
2. What are your hopes and dreams for this year? By the time you graduate from high school?

Prayer

Pray that God will help you to lead your child by example, walking the path of righteousness He has set before you as a parent. Pray that God will give your child peace during times of anxiety he may face in his daily life. Promise to continually pray for him as he encounters daily challenges.

Child:

Thank you for talking to me about your experiences when you matured from childhood to a young adult. Sometimes I think I am the only one who has ever felt this way. It helps me to know you have been through these same changes. When I think about the next year, I feel afraid about (share your worries, fears, or concerns about the future). Right now I feel good about (share any comfort, peace, or joy you feel at this moment).

Questions to Ask Your Parent

1. Do you remember a time when you were my age that you were afraid or anxious about something?
2. What did you do about it?

Testimony:

I still remember when the big day arrived for my wife, Cathy, to take Christy (our oldest) on an overnight trip. Cathy was going to talk to Christy about puberty and all the changes taking place in her body and life. We had chosen a book to read about sexuality that was age appropriate. Christy really didn't understand what she was in for. She just knew she was going on an outing with her mom. They were staying in a cool hotel next to a mall where she was going to get a brand-new outfit—plus, she wouldn't have to compete with her sisters for time with Mom.

As Cathy began to talk about preparing for adolescence, Christy actually engaged in the conversation. Cathy called me later and excitedly told me how wonderful the conversation had been. It was one of those parent-child milestones that made a real difference.

Two years later Cathy did the same thing with our daughter Rebecca, and then again two years later with Heidi. Rebecca was thrilled to do the overnight and get the outfit. She chose to have absolutely no dialogue with her mom about any of "that gross stuff." Heidi's time with Cathy had more dialogue, but her big sisters had already filled her in on puberty! As my girls—now grown women— look back on those special trips, they all agree that however awkward it may have felt at the time, the conversations had a profound and lasting effect on their passage through puberty and their perspective on sexuality.

A sixth grader's dad

Laying the Foundation of Faith

One of the most common hallmarks of the sixth-grade year is a sudden development of self-consciousness. Children become insecure and unsure of themselves, almost overnight. There are more and more questions they can't answer, especially issues of social justice and faith. Often they begin to wonder if they are special in any way, and they may find it hard to believe that they can do anything well.

The expression of these feelings—whether verbally or through emotional swings—is your cue to point your child to God's love and acceptance. Your goal is to help him see that his life and purpose were conceived in the beautiful imagination of God the Creator. You want your child to look at how he is shaped and wired and experience a deep sense of wonder. Ultimately, he should grasp two important truths:

1. God, in His great creativity and wisdom, created everything—including him. Your child is fearfully and wonderfully made!

   For you created my inmost being;
       you knit me together in my mother's
       womb.

I praise you because I am fearfully and
    wonderfully made;
  your works are wonderful,
  I know that full well.
My frame was not hidden from you
  when I was made in the secret place,
  when I was woven together in the depths
    of the earth.
Your eyes saw my unformed body;
  all the days ordained for me were written
    in your book
  before one of them came to be.
    (Ps. 139:13–16)

2. When change happens and life is hard, God is still there. He is strong even when your child doesn't feel strong. He is big enough to handle the tough stuff— even puberty!

Do you not know?
  Have you not heard?
The LORD is the everlasting God,
  the Creator of the ends of the earth.
He will not grow tired or weary,
  and his understanding no one can fathom.
He gives strength to the weary
  and increases the power of the weak.
Even youths grow tired and weary,

and young men stumble and fall;
but those who hope in the LORD
will renew their strength.
They will soar on wings like eagles;
they will run and not grow weary,
they will walk and not be faint.
(Isa. 40:28–31)

Sixth grade is the next step in the quest to leave a legacy of faith to your child. The best way to end the adolescent journey well is to begin it well. That's why it is so important to lay a solid foundation now, even if your eleven- or twelve-year-old still seems like a little kid. The bond you build this year can last a lifetime and help launch your child into successful adulthood.

Since puberty plays such a big role in this stage of development, it needs to be your main focus of discussion. It may not seem fun to talk about puberty, but it's much less fun to have your child learn from someone else or to leave him alone to figure it out via friends or the Internet. In this stage of parenting you must begin a habit of greater openness in your relationship. Part of creating a beautiful connection with your child is being willing to share some of your own memories and lessons from puberty, even when it's uncomfortable. Again, your occasional discomfort in explaining puberty is far better than the alternative methods of learning available to your child in this era of cell phones and Internet access.

Parenting does not have to be about survival. God has called you to shepherd and lead one of His children through a critical and life-changing season of life. What an amazing and exciting responsibility! God's desire is not for both of you to merely survive; rather, He wants to see you thrive through this transition.

What You Need to Know about Sixth Graders

Around this time in most children's development, the brain begins to release hormones—lots and lots of hormones. These hormones initiate a host of physical, mental, and emotional changes commonly known as puberty. Puberty is a unique time in all of our lives. Some people breeze through it and others have a tougher time with emotions or physical changes. While it is true that children become more emotional and self-conscious at this age, they also begin to develop social awareness, express their feelings more frequently, and move from concrete thinking to more abstract thinking. As a parent, you can take advantage of these changes to create opportunities for spiritual and character formation.

Physically, sixth graders:

- Receive an internal "hormone cocktail" that kick-starts puberty and prepares the body to begin the process of growing into adulthood
- May experience hormones being released inconsistently, causing drastic mood swings
- May experience a high energy level that is balanced by an increased need for rest

- May experience their bones and muscles growing at different rates, leading to feelings of awkwardness and clumsiness
- Need to pay attention to personal hygiene

In addition, boys:

- May begin to grow facial and pubic hair and notice their voices cracking and sounding deeper

In addition, girls:

- Will typically experience growth spurts before boys and may grow pubic hair, develop breasts, and start their periods

Emotionally, sixth graders:

- Become moody and easily frustrated
- Experiment with off-color humor and silliness
- Show more concern for body image
- Begin to express feelings more frequently
- Experience emotions in extremes
- Are characterized by curiosity
- Become more socially expansive and aware
- Express less affection for parents
- Encounter periods of sadness, depression, and desperation, which can lead to poor coping habits

Relationally, sixth graders:

- Undergo changes in their friendships due to new schools, boyfriends/girlfriends, and changes of affinity groups
- Experience wild mood swings that can cause turmoil in their friendships
- May struggle with being rejected by a friend or left out of a group of friends

In addition, boys:

- Tend to build friendships in packs of eight to ten, based on affinity, yet some struggle with being loners if they do not find a pack of friends

In addition, girls:

- Tend to build friendships in groups of two to three

Spiritually, sixth graders:

- Begin to move from concrete to abstract thinking, which creates a new world of questions about faith and spiritual things

- Question and disagree with parents' beliefs, but are tamed by fear to express those doubts
- Develop a major concern about how God can help them in their daily lives
- Struggle to see the relevance of the Bible in their lives
- Learn through relationships with significant adults; spiritual lessons are more caught than taught

8

Seventh Grade: The Blessing

During the seventh-grade year, most kids will celebrate their thirteenth birthday. Turning thirteen is an important milestone—not only in the life of a child but also in culture as a whole. It is a special season of life uniquely positioned between childhood and adulthood.

At one time, age thirteen actually represented one's entrance into adulthood. Can you imagine your seventh grader taking on full adult responsibilities? Maybe the teenage years aren't so bad after all!

Consider some examples from civilizations around the world. In many tribal systems, boys turning thirteen are sent into the jungle to survive for three days with no provisions. Upon their return, the entire tribe gathers to celebrate their transition into manhood. Other tribes require boys to undergo rites that inflict pain or complete a series of military or physical tests in order to assess their readiness for adulthood. In some cultures, a thirteen-year-old girl is chosen as the future bride of a young man, all arranged by their parents. Orthodox Jews mark the thirteenth birthday as significant with a bar mitzvah (boys) or bat mitzvah (girls) in which family and friends gather for a large celebration acknowledging the young person's new rights and responsibilities within the community.

Although traditions vary, these cultural rites share the same intent: marking the transition from childhood into adulthood. It's probably not a good idea to send your child alone into the wilderness or to test her physical strength with dangerous experiences. However, it is important to acknowledge her readiness for greater challenges and responsibilities. The seventh-grade year provides an unparalleled opportunity to educate and inspire your child to make the most of the years ahead. In fact, it is the perfect time to give your child the gift of a blessing.

Jeremy's Story

I am from Baltimore, Maryland.

If you live in Baltimore, it is practically a legal requirement to be a fan of Cal Ripken Jr., the legendary shortstop for the Baltimore Orioles. In fact, if you are from Baltimore, you will always remember where you were on the night of September 6, 1995—the night Cal Ripken played his 2,131st game and broke the fifty-six-year-old Major League Baseball record for consecutive games. I was sitting in my dorm room at Mississippi College in Clinton, glued to the television. I was sad to be viewing this historic event without my family in Maryland.

The next morning when I checked my email, there was a note in my inbox from my dad.

Dear Jonathan [my older brother, who was copied on the email] and Jeremy,
    Last night, I watched Cal Ripken Jr. break the big record. He was doing a lap around the stadium shaking the fans' hands and celebrating.

Then they turned the camera to Cal Sr. in the dugout. [Cal Jr.'s dad was a coach on the team.]

I lost it.

I started crying, not because of Cal Jr. breaking the record, but because in that moment I realized that I have two Hall of Fame sons who will make more of a difference in this world than any broken record could.

I am so proud of the men you have become. I love you.

Dad

Ninety-eight words. That email from my dad contained only ninety-eight words, but they were a gift unlike any other I will ever receive. Those ninety-eight words constituted my father's blessing, and it will forever affect me.

Seventh Grade Rite of Passage
Ceremony: The blessing ceremony
Symbol: The blessing

At the center of the seventh grade Rite of Passage Experience is the blessing ceremony. The blessing is designed to recognize and celebrate your child's exit from childhood and the beginning of her transition into adulthood. The ceremony can coincide with the celebration of her thirteenth birthday, or it can be held at another time during the year that works for your family and friends.

One of the key elements of the blessing ceremony is to discuss it with your child in advance. It is important for her to understand that she has no choice whether or not she receives a blessing, but she does have a choice in *how* she receives it. Below are three options for bestowing a blessing:

1. **A written blessing.** This is a letter from you to your child that includes a specific blessing. You will give it to your child, and then she will read it in private. This is an excellent option for a shy or extremely introverted teen.

2. **A family dinner.** Host a dinner for your child and any other family members or friends she chooses to invite. Serve your child's favorite foods. During the dinner, one or both parents will give a blessing and offer other special guests an opportunity to do the same.

3. **A public blessing.** If your teenager is very social or extroverted, a party might be the perfect venue for her blessing ceremony. In this setting, preparing the blessing in advance to read aloud at the event is encouraged. We have experienced several blessing parties where families came together with significant people in their thirteen-year-olds' lives. At these parties, affirmations and blessings from guests were given to the guest of honor in front of everyone. After all the blessings were given, guests gathered to pray for the child. One of the most significant blessing ceremonies I (Jim) was ever a part of was when a letter was read from the young man's grandpa who had passed away the month before. There was not a dry eye in the room.

What is a blessing? It is an opportunity to build courage in your teenager through encouragement and to create a spiritual marker in her life. A blessing is not a time to instruct your teenager on what you wish she would change or do better. It is also not about what your child has accomplished or what her goals in life should be, but rather an affirmation of who (and whose) she is. As a parent, you know the heart of your teenager better than anyone else on the planet. The blessing is a time for you to hold up a mirror to her soul and explain who she is, not just what she has done.

A blessing should affirm your teenager's identity. Don't be afraid to mention accomplishments, but do not make achievement the foundation of the blessing. Consider phrases such as the ones below:

- I know you to be a kind person who takes care of those in need.
- I marvel at how patient you are. I want you to know that I see you are slow to become angry, and I admire that.
- One of the things I respect the most is a hard worker, and when I watch you, I see a very hard worker.
- When you walk into a room, you light it up. You have been given the gift of charisma—you shine from your soul for others to see.
- I appreciate how you think before you speak. You are a deep thinker, and that is going to serve you well in life.

A blessing should affirm your teenager's faith.

- Scripture pierces the outer core and goes straight to the heart. When preparing a blessing, include a verse that means a lot to you or that reminds you of your child and her walk with the Lord.

- Use a symbol. Whatever character trait you are seeking to validate or encourage in your child can be represented by a symbol. If you present her with the symbol during her blessing, it will be a powerful reminder for the rest of her life. (We've seen artwork, a Bible, a devotional book, a Christian CD, and many others.)

- Pray for your child; prayer is a powerful tool. Intercede on behalf of your child, give testimony to God's faithfulness, and express thanks for God's love and provision.

A blessing should affirm your teenager's choices. This part of the blessing is a time to compare your child to someone she knows and admires or to introduce her to someone new. It is a powerful opportunity to develop a hero in your child's life and provide a tangible example of someone who lives out an attribute you are ascribing to your child. Consider these statements:

- You remind me of your grandfather. He was one of the kindest men I have ever met. I

sometimes have to do a double take when I
see the way you love people. It looks so much
like the way he respected and honored people.

- Martin Luther King Jr. was a man of peace.
  When the whole world wanted to respond
  to racism in violence, he taught a nation to
  respond with love. I see a similar spirit of
  peace in you.

- In the Bible there is a man named Joshua.
  He was known to be a man of great courage.
  I often look at you and see that same kind of
  courage.

A blessing should affirm your teenager's future. Inspire her
and help her believe something about herself that she might have
otherwise overlooked. Hidden within each blessing is a golden
opportunity to guide your teenager and help her dream. Consider
these examples:

- My dream for you in the coming year is that
  you will continue to grow in your love for
  others, that you will find ways to serve those
  around you, and that you will use your abilities to make others smile.

- My dream for you is that you will be a peace-
  maker. You have a calming presence about
  you that can be a great attribute to your
  friends when they experience conflict.

- I am so excited to watch you throughout this next year as you take your hard-work ethic and apply it to your life through school, sports, and other activities. There is no telling what will happen when you put such extraordinary effort into all you do. I am proud of you.

- My dream for you this year is that you will find ways to use your gift of leadership, which is so evident.

Testimony:

We attended the Pass It On Rites of Passage Experience training that was hosted by our church. This training opened our eyes as parents to new experiences we could have with our sons—ones we had never thought of before. Immediately we decided to do the blessing for Joshua who was going to turn thirteen that year. Joshua didn't want to have a birthday party when he turned twelve, because he felt he was getting too old for a party. The ironic thing is he asked for a party this year. He said since he was turning thirteen, he felt it was an important age.

This worked out perfectly for us to present the blessing during his party. Joshua told us his gift could be his party; however, the one gift he truly wanted was a purity ring.

I used the Blessing Worksheet to develop what I wanted to say to Joshua. During the party we had everyone gather around, and we gave Joshua a box, which contained a plaque. Joshua's second gift was his purity ring.

I explained to everyone about the Rites of Passage Experience training my wife and I had attended at church. Then I read verses from Proverbs 1:8 and 1 John 3:16 to my son, while he stood next to his mother.

Today Joshua has the plaque hung up on his wall. Our next Rites of Passage Experience will be with our older son (Justin) before he begins to drive. Here's the blessing that we had imprinted on Joshua's plaque:

Joshua, I wanted to take a few moments today to tell you how important you are to me. I am so proud of the person you have become. You are very passionate, caring, and intelligent. In fact, you remind me of your mother.

The verses I want to read to you that remind me of who God made you to be are Proverbs 1:8 and 1 John 3:16.

My dream for you in the next year of your life is that you follow your heart in all you do. That you know God is in all the small details that make you so perfect. I wanted to give you this symbol that represents the promise God has for those who follow His plan. When you look at it, I want you to always remember what I believe to be true about who you are and your love for the Lord.

I love you. I am proud of you.

A seventh grader's dad

Laying the Foundation of Faith

Speaking a blessing over your child is not a new concept. In fact, blessings are prevalent in God's story. There are more than seven hundred references to blessings in the Bible. In God's design, He tasked the family as the primary source for telling His story. The blessing was the vehicle for releasing the next generation to live in that story. Take time to read and meditate on these stories of blessing.

- Genesis 1:22: the first blessing
- Genesis 12: a blessing with a challenge
- Genesis 27: a blessing that did not go as planned, but was still used by God
- Genesis 37: an imperfect blessing used by God
- Luke 2:25–38: a blessing spoken over Jesus

Imparting a blessing to your child unleashes her to discover God's unique plan for her. It serves as a critical bridge between the practical lessons of parenting and the spiritual inheritance you desire to instill in her. A blessing gives your child confidence to seek greater understanding of God and embrace deeper commitments with Him and others. It is a catalyst to her quest for personal, authentic faith.

> For through wisdom your days will be many,
>   and years will be added to your life.
> If you are wise, your wisdom will reward you;
>   if you are a mocker, you alone will suffer.
>   (Prov. 9:11–12)

"But what about you?" he asked. "Who do you say I am?"

> Simon Peter answered, "You are the Messiah,
> the Son of the living God." (Matt. 16:15–16)

In the midst of a child's struggle to find meaning and identity, a parent can step in to say, "You have my approval. I believe in who you are—not just what you do. You are special to me, and I love you. Now go out into the world and make a difference. God has a plan for your life, and I can't wait to see it unfold."

What You Need to Know about Seventh Graders

The seventh-grade year is heavily influenced by judgments and comparisons. Because kids at this age continue to develop and grow at various rates, differences are usually obvious. Technology and social media usage become more prevalent, and sports and extracurricular activities play a role in social circles. As students experience heightened awareness of the changes in their bodies and the people around them, the number of insecurities they feel increase. They seek value in friendships, sports, or clubs and may go to great lengths to be accepted.

Physically, seventh graders:

- May be subjected to comparisons by other students who are developing faster or slower
- May experience a high energy level that is balanced by an increased need for rest

- May have skin problems, such as acne, that can become an issue
- May experience bones and muscles growing at different rates, leading to feelings of awkwardness and clumsiness
- Pay more attention to personal hygiene

In addition, girls:

- Typically experience growth spurts one year ahead of boys and most have begun menstruating

Emotionally, seventh graders:

- Desire and need more privacy
- Become moody and easily frustrated
- Begin to stress about relationships and increased schoolwork
- Begin to experience bullying issues
- Show more concern about body image
- Experience emotions in extremes
- Are more curious
- Become more socially expansive and aware
- Express less affection toward parents
- Encounter periods of sadness, depression, and desperation, which can lead to poor coping habits

Relationally, seventh graders:

- Can be emotionally damaged by adults who tease them
- Carry a strong desire to be accepted by peers
- Experience changes in their friendships due to new schools, boyfriends/girlfriends, and change of affinity groups
- Want to own and overuse a cell phone
- Might have a strong interest in sports

In addition, boys:

- Tend to build friendships in packs of eight to ten, based on affinity
- Struggle with being loners if they do not find a pack of friends

In addition, girls:

- Have a tendency to be interested in older boys
- Tend to build friendships in groups of two to three

Spiritually, seventh graders:

- Have a great ability to memorize scriptures but still struggle to understand them

- Thrive in a small peer group led by a trusted adult who serves as a spiritual guide
- Begin to pave the way toward abstract thinking from the concrete, which creates a new world of questions about faith and spiritual matters
- May question and disagree with their parents' beliefs, but are tamed by fear to express those doubts
- Are learning how parents interact with God through prayer and are ready to practice daily Bible study (with parental encouragement)
- Are ready to take on difficult intellectual tasks

9

Eighth Grade: Purity Code Weekend*

You should not have a sex talk with your teenager. A one-time lecture with your teenager about sex is pretty much a waste of time. However, an *ongoing dialogue* with your teen on this important subject is critical to helping him make wise choices and have a healthy, God-honoring view of sexuality. Experts on the subject (both Christian and secular) agree: the more positive, healthy, value-centered conversations kids have about sex at home, the less promiscuous they will be. We strongly believe your conversations should focus on the concept of purity.

Chances are good that your parents did not equip you to deal with this issue. In fact, many people have never witnessed a properly modeled parenting example of how it should look to discuss sex and purity. It is almost guaranteed that your child has heard about sex from other people. What if, instead of avoiding the topic and hoping he figures it out, you use this opportunity to expand his view of sex to a biblical understanding of purity? You can proactively address the distorted misinformation he has gleaned from peers and Hollywood and provide him with an educated, mature framework from which to consider this topic.

You have the opportunity to blaze a new trail by putting your child on a path of sexual purity that could potentially save him from some of the greatest heartaches teenagers encounter. Take a deep breath. You can do it. Although it seems intimidating, your efforts will have an impact on your teenager and family for generations to come.

* We suggest that you start teaching your child healthy sexuality between the ages of three and five, then again between the ages of six and nine to talk about more issues.[1] Around age ten is when he will begin experiencing the first signs of puberty. And again, this is when you engage in conversations about another new phase. The Purity Code Weekend is not intended to be a one-shot conversation about sexuality.

Eighth Grade Rite of Passage
Ceremony: Purity code weekend
Symbol: Purity ring or other gift

The eighth grade Rite of Passage Experience centers on purity. Because this conversation has the potential to be awkward, we suggest that the discussion of sex and purity takes place during a fun weekend trip or event.[2] The first step is to plan your trip—with the help of your teen. It is most effective for the event to take place with one parent and one teenager, such as a father/son or mother/daughter experience. It doesn't have to always be a same-sex parent/

child conversation; many single parents do a great job with different genders. The most important part is to give the gift of a Purity Code Weekend. Individual circumstances will dictate what this weekend looks like, so be flexible and creative. It's not about the amount of money spent or the distance traveled; it is about the investment in your child.

Before the weekend begins, share the specific time you plan to discuss sex and purity with your teenager. By notifying him in advance, he will not be surprised and will have time to prepare. Make sure to choose a place that is both private and comfortable for both of you.

When talking about purity or any sexually related topic, you should initiate the conversation but refrain from lecturing. Consider sharing your own experiences in learning about the subject of sex, including the positive and negative aspects, as well as the ways it affected you as an adult. Share your dreams for your child in the area of sexual purity and encourage him to develop a dream of his own. Most parents appreciate using a book, CD, or curriculum to make it easier to have the conversation. One source for finding books on healthy sexuality is the Pure Foundation Series.[3]

The Purity Code Weekend

This weekend is a great time to review what the Bible says about marriage and purity. Consider using the following Scripture verses:

- Genesis 1:26 and 31 remind us that God sees sex as a good thing.

Then God said, "Let us make mankind in our image, in our likeness, so that they may rule over the fish in the sea and the birds in the sky, over the livestock and all the wild animals, and over all the creatures that move along the ground." … God saw all that he had made, and it was very good. And there was evening, and there was morning—the sixth day."

- Exodus 20:14 tells us not to commit adultery.

  "You shall not commit adultery."

- First Thessalonians 4:3 gives us God's standard for sex.

  "It is God's will that you should be sanctified: that you should avoid sexual immorality."

- Matthew 19:4–6 teaches that God created man and woman to become one flesh.

  "Haven't you read," he replied, "that at the beginning the Creator 'made them male and female,' and said, 'For this reason a man will leave his father and mother and be united to his wife, and the two will become one flesh'? So they are no longer two, but one flesh. Therefore what God has joined together, let no one separate."

- First Corinthians 6:18–20 reminds us to honor God with our bodies and sexuality.

"Flee from sexual immorality. All other sins a person commits are outside the body, but whoever sins sexually, sins against their own body. Do you not know that your bodies are temples of the Holy Spirit, who is in you, whom you have received from God? You are not your own; you were bought at a price. Therefore honor God with your bodies."

Many people in our culture ridicule the idea of waiting until marriage to have sex. Take some time to discuss the common viewpoints against God's plan for sex. Below are some statements that might be helpful in this part of the discussion:

- I have never met someone who waited until marriage to have sex and regretted it. I have also never heard someone say, "I wish I would have had more sex before I was married."
- The people who disagree with God's plan for sex view sex as a physical act rather than an emotional or spiritual commitment. God created sex to connect the body and soul. It is not

designed for casual exchange. Sex for a married couple is like spiritual superglue.

- When you engage in sexual activity prior to marriage, you are creating a marital bond. That type of bond should only follow a marital commitment.

- God's plan for sex is the only safe sex. Using birth control pills or condoms does not guarantee that pregnancy will not occur or that no one will contract a sexually transmitted disease. The only way to completely avoid pregnancy and contracting such a disease is to save sex for its proper place—a committed, monogamous marriage.

- Sex is used to sell movies, music, and products. As a result, sex is undervalued and is often used to satisfy a physical urge at the cost of emotional pain. Rather than viewing sex as only an outlet for pleasure, view it as a valuable treasure to be saved and shared with only your spouse.

- It is your job to honor the purity and integrity of your boyfriend/girlfriend and not take advantage of it. One day you might attend the wedding of someone you once dated. You want to be able to shake the hand of his/her future spouse with no regrets, knowing that you protected his/her purity.

- Most American children see pornography for the first time when they are around eleven.[4] The escalation of pornography has become a

> major issue for teens and adults. God's plan is
> for you to renew your mind for good (see Rom.
> 12:2) and "turn [your] eyes away from worthless
> things" (Ps. 119:37).

Let your teenager know that you value purity in your own life. Give him permission to hold you accountable for treasuring purity in what you watch, what you think, and how you live, and then ask him to commit to purity. To recognize the seriousness of this commitment, give your teenager a symbol to remember it. Some parents give their child a ring that can be exchanged with the wedding ring at the child's future wedding ceremony. Whatever you choose as your symbol, explain how it is special and appropriate for the commitment your child is making.

Before you conclude your discussion, take some time to pray together. Pray that God would guard his mind and fill it with truth, guard his heart and protect it from unnecessary emotional pain, and guard his body from any immorality. Thank God for the gift of sex within the boundaries of marriage and pray for the strength and commitment needed to save it for that relationship.

Despite your well-laid plans, your teen may throw you a curveball during the weekend. Refer to the Resource section for a list of tough questions teenagers often ask about this topic, along with a biblically based answer for each one. Ultimately, there is no way to avoid a little discomfort in this conversation. However, you can quickly follow up your face-to-face talk with some shoulder-to-shoulder fun on your weekend adventure! Again, one of the most effective ways to move through this kind of material is to use a resource such as *The Purity Code*.

We, the authors, are well on the way to watching more than one million kids make a commitment to living by the Purity Code.

Resources

Tough questions teenagers ask about sex[5]

What does God say about sex? God is the creator of sex and wants it to be enjoyed within the boundaries He outlined in His Word. A good metaphor for this is a saltwater aquarium. The focus is on the beauty of the coral, the fish, and the lighting. People don't look at a saltwater aquarium and say, "All this glass, metal, and wood is getting in the way." *The boundaries are not the focus; the beauty is.* At the same time, if the boundaries weren't there, then death, brokenness, and chaos would ensue. God gives us boundaries to keep the beauty in, not to keep the fun stuff out. The Bible says:

> May your fountain be blessed,
>> and may you rejoice in the wife of your youth.
> A loving doe, a graceful deer—
>> may her breasts satisfy you always,
>> may you ever be intoxicated with her love.
> Why, my son, be intoxicated with another man's
>> wife?
> Why embrace the bosom of a wayward
>> woman?
> For your ways are in full view of the LORD,
>> and he examines all your paths.

The evil deeds of the wicked ensnare them;
  the cords of their sins hold them fast.
For lack of discipline they will die,
  led astray by their own great folly.
    (Prov. 5:18–23)

What is a sexually transmitted disease (STD)? An STD is spread through sexual contact from an infected person to a noninfected person. Any sexual act that involves a bodily fluid can potentially transmit an STD. This can range from oral sex to intercourse. Types of STDs include chlamydia, gonorrhea, syphilis, herpes, genital warts, hepatitis, and HIV/AIDS. Some effects of these diseases include pain, bleeding, infectious discharges, rashes, burning sensations, blisters, sores, and, in some cases, cancer and death. Currently in America, 350 teens contract a sexually transmitted disease every hour. This is one reason God provides boundaries for sex. He does not want to see His children suffer in ways that are, in most cases, completely preventable.

What is intercourse? In many ways, God created a man's and a woman's body to fit together like puzzle pieces. Intercourse is part of the sexual experience in which the penis of the male is inserted into the vaginal canal of the female.

What is an orgasm? An orgasm is another experience that God created for a husband and wife to share. At a certain point in the sexual experience, the body releases chemicals called endorphins into the body. These chemicals cause a person to feel a sense of euphoria, joy, and intense excitement called an orgasm.

What is oral sex, and does God consider it to be sex? Oral sex is when one person stimulates the other person's genitals with his or her mouth. God does consider this to be sex, because it is a process that affects a person physically, emotionally, and spiritually.

What is pornography? Pornography is any portrayal of nudity or sexual experience, be it video, audio, pictorial, or written. Pornography, at its core, causes people to be viewed as objects of lust rather than the beautiful creations God intended them to be. It trains people to look upon the opposite sex disrespectfully, and it causes people to "lust in their hearts" (see Matt. 5:28), as Jesus taught against in the Sermon on the Mount. Addiction to pornography occurs in stages:

- viewing pornography
- addiction
- escalation
- desensitization
- acting out sexually

Marriages are destroyed because of this. Because pornography is so readily available, monitoring software (such as www.covenanteyes.com or www.xxxchurch.com) can provide an extra level of accountability for teens and their families.

What is sexting, and is it okay? Sexting involves sending messages that describe sexual acts or sending nude pictures or videos of one-self to other people via text or instant messaging. Although it can seem harmless, sexting is often used to manipulate the person who received the message into doing things he or she does not want to do. Also, by sending these types of messages, the person is inviting lust and possible immoral behavior into the lives of the ones to whom the images are sent. This is definitely not God's will for anyone. Last, it is very possible that the person who receives the message will share it with his or her friends, using it as a tool to cause shame and embarrassment for the person who sent it.

What is …? Because there is no way to anticipate every question you will be asked, you need to be armed with the silver-bullet answer that will get you out of just about any question you can't answer. Are you ready for it? The answer is, "I don't know. Let's explore it together!" It's that simple. Just admit to your teenager that you don't know the best way to answer his question, but you will find an answer or work with him to find it. Then you can follow through on your promise.

Ideas for striving for God's best in relationships

- Ask fearless questions such as, "How are you doing in this relationship?"
- Introduce your teen to couples who have powerful purity stories they are willing to share with your child.
- Point out scriptures that reinforce trusting God's best for our lives.

- Discourage your middle-school-aged child from dating, and have him wait until at least his junior year of high school to date.
- Teach your son to call and ask a girl's father if he can ask her out on a date, to get better acquainted and to keep the lines of communication open.
- If your teen is in a relationship, have dinner with the young couple once a month.
- Sexting is a HUGE problem among teens, so social media accountability is nonnegotiable. You should always be allowed to know passwords and check your teen's text messages and Facebook, Twitter, Snapchat, and Instagram accounts.

Laying the Foundation of Faith

First teach your teen the Purity Code:

In honor of God, my family, and my future spouse, I commit to sexual purity.

This involves

- honoring God with your body;
- renewing your mind for good;
- turning your eyes from worthless things; and
- guarding your heart.

Committing to and living by the Purity Code is rooted in Scripture and deepens your teen's commitment to God.

When explaining the sacredness of sex, a good thing to say is that God *intends* for us to be joined and united as one with another human being. Sexual intimacy was always part of His plan for us! Take a look at the passage below from Genesis 2.

> Then the LORD God made a woman from the rib
> he had taken out of the man, and he brought her
> to the man.
>
> The man said,
> "This is now bone of my bones
>   and flesh of my flesh;
> she shall be called 'woman,'
>   for she was taken out of man."
>
> That is why a man leaves his father and mother
> and is united to his wife, and they become one
> flesh. Adam and his wife were both naked, and
> they felt no shame. (vv. 22–25)

When God first brought man and woman together, Adam was amazed to realize that Eve was, literally, a part of him. Leaving the family unit in which you were raised and becoming one with another person was conceived in the heart of God. It is a solemn sacrifice to care for another person physically, emotionally, spiritually, and sexually. God did not intend for it to be carelessly repeated with different people throughout our lives.

Grace and restoration play an important part in this discussion, because our kids sometimes stumble and make poor choices in the area of sex. Our lives are not perfect either, as married couples often struggle and separate, or even divorce. Still, we must help our teens strive to experience one flesh with just one person, guarding their hearts in a world of broken ones.

Intimacy

Another important component of a God-honoring relationship is intimacy. Intimacy enables you to let down your guard and be authentic, without the fear of rejection. You can experience a variety of intimate relationships in life—with a close friend, a family member, and, hopefully, your relationship with Christ. Consider these examples in the Bible:

> After David had finished talking with Saul, Jonathan became one in spirit with David, and he loved him as himself. (1 Sam. 18:1)

> His left arm is under my head
>   and his right arm embraces me....
> Place me like a seal over your heart,
>   like a seal on your arm;
> for love is as strong as death. (Song of Sol. 8:3, 6)

> As she stood behind him at his feet weeping, she began to wet his feet with her tears. Then she wiped

> them with her hair, kissed them and poured perfume on them. (Luke 7:38)

Intimacy ultimately results in a feeling of belongingness and safety within a relationship marked by unconditional love. It should be pursued with fervor and protected with intensity.

God's best

Although it's true that sex outside of marriage is a bad choice, sex is still God's gift to us. It's not helpful to just tell your teen that sex is bad. Rather than trying to scare your child into waiting or focusing on the consequences of promiscuity, help your child see sex as a gift he can save and give his spouse on their wedding night. Read the following verses:

> Adam and his wife were both naked, and they felt no shame. (Gen. 2:25)

> But you are a chosen people, a royal priesthood, a holy nation, God's special possession, that you may declare the praises of him who called you out of darkness into his wonderful light. (1 Pet. 2:9)

God has His very best in mind for us when He commands us to save sex for marriage. That's why your teen should be concerned about not only what God wants for him but also what God desires for the people to whom he is attracted or over whom he has influence. When he learns to view sex through the lens of God's best, he will realize that his sexual behavior has an impact on other people too.

Practical steps

> As for other matters, brothers and sisters, we instructed you how to live in order to please God, as in fact you are living. Now we ask you and urge you in the Lord Jesus to do this more and more. For you know what instructions we gave you by the authority of the Lord Jesus.
>
> It is God's will that you should be sanctified: that you should avoid sexual immorality; that each of you should learn to control your own body in a way that is holy and honorable, not in passionate lust like the pagans, who do not know God; and that in this matter no one should wrong or take advantage of a brother or sister. (1 Thess. 4:1–6)

In the passage above, Paul reminds the church in Thessalonica that he has given them a description of how to walk with and please God. Christian culture does a good job of telling teens, "Don't do that" when it comes to sex. Unfortunately, we often neglect the job of equipping them for that challenge and what to replace their desire with. It's important to give our children practical guidance to help them set healthy boundaries in their relationships.

Encourage your teen to enjoy co-ed friendship in groups as often as possible. Sharing everyday experiences with members of the opposite sex through friendship can often teach your child a lot more than a typical dating relationship will. Make sure to establish PDA (public display of affection) boundaries in your home to help him avoid tempting situations. Where in the house is your teen allowed to hang out with friends of the opposite sex? How much privacy can he expect to have? Laying clear and consistent ground rules before the occasion arises will ease tension and avoid additional conflict. Throughout these coming years, maintain an open dialogue about upholding God's best in his dating life and how to navigate difficult situations.

Sex and purity conversations can be the hardest ones to have with your teen, but they are also opportunities to take your relationship to a new level. Your child may wince every time you say the word "sex," but he really does want to feel safe discussing this topic with you. Remember that no one has a louder voice than you in the life of your teenager. Your words—and actions—matter! Although it is hard and sometimes uncomfortable, you are using your influence to set him up for success and health in the area of sex. You are ensuring he has the biblical and intellectual foundation to place purity at the center of his relationships. That is truly one of the best investments you will ever make.

Testimony:

My husband took our son on a camping and fishing trip right before he started his eighth-grade year. Our son is "all boy," and this was a great time to be with his dad. My husband had told him they were also going to talk about the Purity Code. He told his dad that would be "weird and awkward," and he wasn't interested in having a talk about sex, relationships, or girls. This caused my husband to lose confidence that they could have some discussion about the Purity Code.

He had never had his dad or mom talk to him about anything related to sex. But they went on the trip and my husband brought the Purity Code book he was hoping to go over with our son. Each night my husband would read chapters on his own while our son did other things around the campfire.

Finally on the last night, our son asked his dad what he was reading. He said it was the book for students about the Purity Code. Our son asked, "What's it say?" They ended up talking about really personal stuff for over two hours by the campfire. They decided when they got back home they would go through the book and go out for fun food each week.

I'm not sure who had a better experience, my son or my husband. But this I do know—their relationship is definitely different, and our son committed to those Purity Code words: "In honor of God, my family, and my future spouse, I commit to sexual purity." Our son didn't want a purity ring, but we gave him a really cool painting of a young boy and his dad fly-fishing in a stream in the mountains as a reminder of that special decision he made to remain sexually pure.

An eighth grader's mom

What You Need to Know about Eighth Graders

Sometime during the eighth grade, most teenagers say good-bye to puberty issues and hello to the quest for freedom from parents and childish things. Girls have almost fully developed physically by this time, but boys usually have at least one more growth spurt to complete. At this age, boys tend to hang out in large groups or packs of eight to ten, while girls gather in smaller groups of two to three. You will probably also experience some big changes in the parent-child relationship.

Teenagers are notorious for treating most conversations as a negotiation for something they want. They begin to question authority, analyze the behavior of adults, and may even conclude they know more than the adults they encounter—including you! At the same time, your teenager is looking for spiritual leaders who will dialogue with him rather than lecture him as he explores the issues of faith and belief. All of these behaviors are part of his quest to solidify his identity and find his place—at home, at school, and with friends.

That's why this year is the perfect time to talk to your child about purity. He needs to understand God's design for relationships and marriage, as well as the importance of intimacy, before he finds himself in a delicate or difficult situation.

Physically, eighth graders:

- Level out in height
- Will most likely be fully awakened to sexual desire
- Have a need to develop exercise routines and healthy habits

In addition, boys:

- Begin to develop upper-body strength
- Will continue to grow—possibly all the way through high school

In addition, girls:

- Are almost fully developed physically

Emotionally, eighth graders:

- Have a more evident adult personality
- Want to try new things in an effort to discover identity
- Obtain a strong sense of accomplishment from being involved in various activities
- Are easily bored
- Begin to question authority and analyze their own behavior
- Exhibit impulsive behavior with friends and peers
- Express less affection for parents
- Don't respond to adult lectures, feeling they know better about what is going on than adults do
- Experience periods of sadness, depression, and desperation, which can lead to poor coping habits if unchecked

Relationally, eighth graders:

- Focus on negotiation with parents to get what they want
- Have a strong desire to be accepted by their peers

- Want to own and overuse a cell phone
- Experience changes in their friendships due to new schools, boyfriends/girlfriends, and change of affinity groups
- Might have a strong interest in sports

In addition, boys:

- Tend to build friendships in packs of eight to ten, based on affinity
- Struggle with being loners if they do not find a pack of friends

In addition, girls:

- Have a tendency to be interested in older boys
- Tend to build friendships in groups of two to three

Spiritually, eighth graders:

- Need a trusted and loving adult to talk with them about what the Bible teaches on subjects such as sex
- Need spiritual leaders to ask them for their opinions so they can develop their beliefs rather than be told what to believe

- Vacillate on their interest in and commitment to faith, signaling internal struggle about whether to accept it
- Enjoy studying the Bible and are ready to begin the practice daily (with a lot of encouragement), though they are timid about taking on difficult intellectual tasks

10

Ninth Grade: Driving Contract

Often when you are approaching a big life event, the very thought of it instantly elicits both fear and excitement. That's what happens when your teenager approaches driving age. She is excited about the thought of freedom, unlimited social opportunities, and the potential of driving a car! All you can think about is how afraid you are to allow her to drive a car. Even though a typical ninth grader is not old enough to get a driver's license yet, age fourteen to fifteen is the right time to celebrate this rite of passage—well before you take her to the Department of Motor Vehicles.

Have you ever considered that putting your teenager behind the wheel of a car is not really about driving? It is about the upcoming driving experience, signifying much more than horsepower and mobility. Driving results in a dramatic shift in the parent-child relationship. As a driver, your teenager will spend an increasing amount of time away from you, giving her a significant amount of freedom for the first time. This newfound freedom gives you the opportunity to gauge her moral compass. How will she handle making decisions when she's away from you? Will she be safe? Will she fail miserably? Will she surprise you?

What if you used the upcoming driving experience to give your teenager something more important than the keys to your car? Instead of making the experience about obtaining a driver's license, what if you made it about obtaining your trust? Imagine the difference that could make in the moment when your child pulls out of the driveway for the first time.

Ninth Grade Rite of Passage
Ceremony: Driving discussion
Symbol: Driving contract

The ninth grade Rite of Passage Experience is built around the development of a driving contract you present to your teenager. This driving contract is not about driving or controlling her behavior. It is about establishing a system for your teenager to both build trust and restore trust if it is ever broken with you. You see, what your teenager wants more than anything is freedom. What you want more than anything is for her to be trustworthy and safe. Therefore, if she earns your trust, you are empowered to reward her with freedom.

The driving contract gives you the opportunity to do three important things:

1. Teach your teenager how to safely operate a car
2. Clearly communicate expectations to your teenager regarding driving

3. Establish a system to strengthen your relationship with her through both building and restoring trust

This contract will help you emphasize the weight and responsibility that comes with getting a driver's license. Depending on your state of residence, your teen may be very close to applying for her driver's permit or the time might be two years away. Regardless of when exactly your child will begin driving, it is important to discuss the qualities she needs to possess in order to enjoy the freedom driving brings. She should have integrity and be trustworthy, safety-minded, and responsible, and be able to make sound decisions independently.

Pick a day to present her with the driving contract, and put it on the calendar. Just as she looks forward to getting her permit, she also needs to look forward to having that meeting with you. Using the sample driving contract in the Resource section, draft your own version. Below are tips for success with the contract:

- Communicate to your teenager that the driving contract is mainly about building trust during the driving adventure.
- Completing a driving contract will not magically prevent your teenager from making a mistake while driving, but it will enable clear communication that includes a plan for restoring broken trust.
- Blank spaces are provided in the contract for you to add any expectations. Consider the following issues you may want to address: the fact

that you as the parents—not your teenager—
are owners of the car; the number (if any) of
passengers permitted in the car; racing or reck-
less driving; the volume of the radio; driving
while texting; eating and drinking while driving; or driving when emotional or upset.

- The portion of the contract that deals with
  consequences is blank. Because this is truly to
  be a two-sided conversation, you should allow
  your teenager to participate in creating consequences. Although you will ultimately control
  the result, your teenager will be more likely to
  honor the consequences if she helped create
  them. Teens, like most people, support what
  they help create.

- Do not allow siblings or others to be a part of
  this rite of passage, so you can eliminate distractions and focus exclusively on your soon-to-be
  driver.

- When your teen receives her driver's license,
  ask older friends and family members to write
  her notes, completing the sentence, "The most
  important thing I learned when I first started
  driving was …" or "The stupidest thing I did
  my first year of driving was …" There will be
  some funny and poignant stories that reinforce
  to your teen that others identify with this new
  freedom she has gained.

- Display the driving contract in the house and give a copy to your teenager.
- Remember to follow up and communicate when trust is broken and then restored.
- If at all possible, make sure both parents are part of the contract. If parents are separated or divorced, it would be a huge win to work together to complete this contract with your teenager. It would communicate security to the teenager.
- You may want to review, revise, and re-sign the driving contract each year on your teenager's birthday to make sure it remains relevant.
- Share with your teenager that the leading cause of death among teenagers is auto accidents. It accounts for more than one-third of all teen deaths each year, so it is extremely important that she takes safety seriously.
- It's wise to establish some limits on driving privileges regarding where she may drive and how many passengers are allowed in the car with her. Don't be afraid to set incremental goals that should be met before additional privileges or responsibilities are given.

During the driving contract meeting, review the contract with your teen and add any remaining points you discuss during the meeting. Every teenager is going to make mistakes when learning to drive. Remember to work through the section of the driving contract to list consequences for when trust is broken. Be sure to pray with your child at the end of the meeting.

Testimony:

It's been a couple of years since we did the driving ceremony contract with our daughter. We wish we had done it with our older son. At first we were hesitant to do a driving contract with her because it was before the age she would be driving. We didn't think it would be very important to her. We were wrong. As we started talking about the responsibility and trust of driving a car, our daughter told us she was apprehensive about getting her license.

My husband decided to take her to a school parking lot on a weekend and teach her to drive. (Not sure this was totally legal :)) She drove around the parking lot with her dad. She was thrilled. They then went out for lunch at a local burger place that she likes. By the time she was out of the car, she had texted most of her friends telling them her dad was teaching her to drive. Then toward the end of her ninth-grade year, she helped us create a driving contract.

We had always heard it said, "People support what they help create." So we asked for her input. Since she didn't have a driver's license already, it was easier to come up with the boundaries and expectations. We typed up the contract and all of us signed it. Today she is a safe driver, and, what is more important, we think she learned the principle of being trustworthy. It was a great experience.

A ninth grader's mom

Resource

Sample driving contract

The goal of this contract is to

- clearly communicate the expectations and desires of the parents and the teenager about driving a vehicle;
- allow parents and their teenager to understand that this is a huge opportunity to build trust in their relationship and grow closer;
- make a plan for when trust is broken, so that it can be restored, allowing the relationship between parents and teenager to grow; and
- agree together ahead of time how to handle unexpected events such as speeding tickets, car accidents, or a broken-down car.

In order to build trust in our family and to honor God in our home, I [insert name] agree that I will

- inform my parents where I am when I am away from them by calling or texting;
- observe and obey speed limits and other traffic laws while driving;
- ask permission to drive until my parents choose to no longer require this of me;

- wear my seat belt and require all passengers to do the same;
- never use my cell phone to text, make phone calls, or check social media while driving, so I can stay focused (I will pull over if I need to use any electronic device);
- not use and definitely will not drive under the influence of alcohol or drugs;
- immediately contact my parents if I am in an accident of any kind (even if it seems minor), and I will not leave the scene of the accident unless my parents or the police give me permission;
- inform my parents of any time I am pulled over for warnings, tickets, or any interaction with the police, and I understand that hiding this from them is a breach of trust in our relationship; and
- not allow any other person to drive my car without the permission of my parents.

Both parents and [insert name] agree that if trust is broken, it will be restored. There are two parts to restoring trust: [Insert name] will experience a consequence first, and then he/she will display trustworthy behavior for a set period of time. Once those two trust builders are complete, trust will be restored in the relationship.

Trust Builder #1: What is the agreed-upon consequence of breaking the above agreement?

_____

_____

_____

Trust Builder #2: What is the agreed-upon period of time that [insert name] must display responsible behavior before trust is restored. (Make sure it is a reasonable amount of time that sets the teenager up for success.)

_____

_____

_____

Parent's Signature _____ Date _____

Parent's Signature _____ Date _____

Teenager's Signature _____ Date _____

Laying the Foundation of Faith

Although driving may not seem like a spiritual activity, it is a place where the fruit of your child's faith either shows up … or it doesn't. Driving is one of the first big tests of integrity during this season of life.

The incredibly fun part of being a first-time driver is the immediate freedom it offers. This experience is meant to be awesome, but it is also the time to set forth clear expectations. How your child drives and incorporates your instructions will, in some way, demonstrate her level of trustworthiness. Driving is a chance for her, when she is out of your sight, to show respect for your teaching and prove her obedience to your wishes.

> Whoever can be trusted with very little can also be trusted with much, and whoever is dishonest with very little will also be dishonest with much. (Luke 16:10)

Driving is a test of integrity. Not only is it a time for your teen to show she can do what she has been instructed to do, but it is also a strong indicator of whether she will do what she says she's going to do. Consider and discuss the spiritual connections to driving. Integrity (or lack of it) in this new endeavor shapes your ability as parents to trust your teen with bigger things in the future.

Teens are at a place in life where their knowledge is growing by leaps and bounds. Unfortunately, their level of impulsivity is also at an all-time high. It's the reason adults look back on something they did at sixteen and say with disdain, "That was a *really* dumb thing to do!"

Teens don't like the word *foolish* being attributed to them, but much of the learning they do at school is disconnected from the development of an ability to foresee consequences. The message that something they are about to do is really dumb or foolish does not typically get to the processing area of their brains until something bad happens.

Your teen's ability to process information should shape the way you prepare for the upcoming driving season. Evaluate how well your teen can connect quick decisions with natural consequences. Help her see any patterns of recklessness in other areas of her life, and challenge her to correct those areas before you turn her loose with the keys to the car.

Foolishness is less painful if we recognize it before something bad happens.

> The wise fear the LORD and shun evil, but a fool is hotheaded and yet feels secure. (Prov. 14:16)

The ninth-grade Rite of Passage Experience is more than just teaching your teenager how to operate a vehicle and avoid speeding tickets. You are giving her your trust. Don't miss the parenting opportunity that accompanies developing a driving contract.

What You Need to Know about Ninth Graders

The ninth-grade year signals the beginning of high school and another leap in the adolescent journey. Girls have generally developed physically into their adult bodies, but boys may still continue to grow.

Sexual desire has usually been awakened by this age, so teenagers become more sensitive to their appearance and social standing and may seek to conform. As their minds develop the ability for more abstract thinking, they begin to engage with God and their faith in new ways. They are also more open to camps and mission experiences because of the potential friendships and relationships that can be formed. For the first time, they may begin to consider what life would look like away from parents, leading to thoughts about careers, goals, and college. Of course, one of the most significant developments is the chance to finally get behind the steering wheel.

Physically, ninth graders:

- May have a heightened sensitivity to appearance and its social value
- Are tempted to become sexually active, because their sexual desire is awakened
- Need to develop exercise routines and healthy habits
- Have a proclivity to diet
- Level out in height

In addition, boys:

- Continue developing upper body strength
- Can expect at least one more growth spurt

In addition, girls:

- Have fully developed into their adult bodies

Emotionally, ninth graders:

- Have a desire for more control over aspects of their lives

- Have more evident adult personalities
- Have idealistic viewpoints of the world at large
- Love trying new things in an effort to discover identity
- Obtain a strong sense of accomplishment from involvement in various activities
- Become easily bored
- Exhibit impulsive behavior with friends and peers
- Don't respond to adult lectures, feeling they know what is going on better than the adult does
- Become better at setting and achieving goals

Relationally, ninth graders:

- Spend less time with family and more time with their friends
- Prefer to compete with outside groups rather than with friends
- Negotiate with parents to get what they want
- Have a strong desire to conform with their peers
- Are strongly influenced by popular peers, adults, and celebrities

In addition, girls:

- Have a tendency to be interested in older boys

Spiritually, ninth graders:

- Have increased capacity for self-discipline
- Are spiritually influenced through summer camps and mission experiences because of the peer connections those events create
- Begin to imagine what life would be like as an adult away from parents and begin deciding whether their faith will be a part of their future
- Are able to fully process abstract thoughts, which gives them the ability to engage with God personally
- Need spiritual leaders to ask their opinions and let them develop their beliefs rather than being told what to believe
- May rapidly vacillate about their interest in and commitment to faith, signaling an internal struggle on whether to accept it

11

Tenth Grade: Money Matters

When did you first learn how to balance a checkbook? At what point did you learn the cost of an average mortgage? Who taught you how much a box of cereal should cost? Did anyone show you how to manage credit cards, how to plan for retirement, or how to avoid debt? Hopefully, someone taught you these things, but whether your parents proactively taught you about stewardship and financial principles or you educated yourself in these matters, you now have the chance to pass on wisdom to your teen. Since money is a resource to be used and shared (and is often a source of great conflict), we strongly believe that financial stewardship must be incorporated into a rite of passage before he enters adulthood.

Whether you are adept at managing money or up to your ears in debt, you still have the responsibility to set your teenager up for a biblical, healthy, and practical understanding of money. From philosophical to practical, there are a lot of important lessons to be taught, including the following:

- Where does money come from?
- How do you honor God with your money?
- Why should you work hard?
- Does generosity matter?

This may seem like a monumental task, but this year's Rite of Passage Experience is going to provide a lot of help. You never know, you may even learn some things yourself!

Tenth Grade Rite of Passage
Ceremony: Money matters
Symbol: Bank account

The tenth grade Rite of Passage Experience centers on an intentional and interactive discussion about money, budgets, and stewardship, which concludes with the presentation of your child's own bank account. Set a meeting date with your teenager when you can eliminate distractions, and put it on the calendar.

At your first Money Matters meeting, give your teenager a blank household budget template to complete. (A sample budget sheet is included in the Resource section. If you do not already know the budget for each category, you will need to determine those before the meeting.) The object of this exercise is for your teen to estimate what your household spends monthly in each category. Do not help him with this activity. The point is to determine how financially aware he is of the cost of running and living in a household.

Once he has completed the form, go through the sheet together and provide the correct answers. Discuss discrepancies, ask and answer questions, and explain the different expenses that make up each budget item.

After finishing the exercise, spend some time focusing on God's plan for managing money, including stewardship, tithing, and generosity. Share a personal testimony of how you learned to manage money or some important turning points in your financial journey.

Here are eight biblical principles on money to review with your tenth grader.

1. **Work hard**

Work in a way that honors God. Remember that the ability to work and earn money is a gift from God. Reject the temptation to be lazy.

Whatever you do, work at it with all your heart, as working for the Lord, not for human masters. (Col. 3:23)

2. **Earn money**

It is not wrong to earn money; in fact, God gave you the ability to earn money and the command to work.

Anyone who does not provide for their relatives, and especially for their own household, has denied the faith and is worse than an unbeliever. (1 Tim. 5:8)

3. Give a tithe back to God first

God wants you to recognize that the money you have comes from Him—He gave you the talent and know-how to do a good job. That makes you the steward of His wealth. Giving a tithe is your recognition that you are managing God's money. (The word *tithe* simply means offering 10 percent of your earnings to God.)

"Bring the whole tithe into the storehouse, that there may be food in my house. Test me in this," says the LORD Almighty, "and see if I will not throw open the floodgates of heaven and pour out so much blessing that there will not be room enough to store it." (Mal. 3:10)

4. Save money

When you earn or receive money, you are not meant to spend it immediately or foolishly. Saving a portion of your money is wise.

A good person leaves an inheritance for their children's children, but a sinner's wealth is stored up for the righteous. (Prov. 13:22)

5. Avoid debt

When you are in debt to someone else, you become obligated to him or her. As much as possible, you should remain obligated to God only.

The rich rule over the poor, and the borrower is slave to the lender. (Prov. 22:7)

6. Be generous with God's money

God calls those who follow Him to use their money to build His kingdom. There is joy in giving money as God leads you.

Each of you should give what you have decided in your heart to give, not reluctantly or under compulsion, for God loves a cheerful giver. (2 Cor. 9:7)

7. Be content

The love of money and material things can take over your life and ruin it if you allow it to. Be content with what God gives you, and avoid collecting or coveting too many possessions.

For where your treasure is, there your heart will be also. (Matt. 6:21)

8. Do not let money become your master

Money is a tool to glorify God and build His kingdom. God is your Master, not money. If money becomes what you love the most, it will ruin your life.

No one can serve two masters. Either you will hate the one and love the other, or you will be devoted

to the one and despise the other. You cannot serve
both God and money. (Matt. 6:24)

At the conclusion of this discussion time, present your teenager
with a symbol to help him remember this experience. If he does not
already have a bank account, this is the perfect moment to open one.
If he has maintained an account for some time, consider making
a special deposit or purchasing a stock or a savings bond for him.
Whatever you do, celebrate the occasion and clearly state that you
are proud of your child and that you trust him to manage his money
well according to God's standards. Conclude your time together with
prayer and commit to being a good example of stewardship.

Resources

Monthly budget worksheet

	Estimate	Actual	Difference
Mortgage/Rent			
Cell phone			
Electricity			
Gas			
Water/Sewer			
Cable/TV			
Car payment			
Car insurance			
Gasoline			
Medical expenses			

Groceries			
Dining out			
Clothes			
Child care			
Church/Charity			
Entertainment			
Savings			
Taxes			

Creative ways to teach money matters

- As early as you can, teach your child to give and save money before he spends it.

- As a family, be involved in a ministry to the poor. A weekly or monthly commitment to such an activity will directly affect your entire family's perspective on money.

- Cultivate a spirit of thankfulness—even in the small things.

- If your teen demands something that is really only a want, tell him he needs to leave the room and then reenter with a gracious and humble attitude before he can repeat the request.

- Give your teen one dollar, five dollars, or ten dollars, and challenge him to multiply the money and invest in meeting someone else's need.

- Assign activities or expenses in your teen's life as his responsibility to fund. If he has an expense that is completely his responsibility, he will learn to set priorities in spending.
- Encourage your student to use his own resources to buy or make birthday gifts for siblings and friends.

Laying the Foundation of Faith

Did you know the Bible talks about money more than about any other subject? In fact, there are more than eight hundred verses in the Bible that address the topic of money. Clearly, this topic is important to God.

The key to teaching healthy financial living is to simultaneously communicate that money does and does not matter. Yes, you read that correctly. When it comes to one's purpose and contentment, money shouldn't matter. Take a look at the following scriptures:

> Better a little with righteousness
>   than much gain with injustice. (Prov. 16:8)

> Be still before the LORD
>   and wait patiently for him;
> do not fret when people succeed in their ways,
>   when they carry out their wicked schemes.
>   (Ps. 37:7)

> Therefore I tell you, do not worry about your life,
> what you will eat or drink; or about your body, what
> you will wear. Is not life more than food, and the body
> more than clothes? Look at the birds of the air; they
> do not sow or reap or store away in barns, and yet your
> heavenly Father feeds them. Are you not much more
> valuable than they? Can any one of you by worrying
> add a single hour to your life? (Matt. 6:25–27)

Most likely, you have heard the phrase "I need _____" from your teenager. Whether it is the latest fashion trend or the newest mobile gadget, today's teens live in a world that often confuses wants with needs. As a parent, you can fall into that trap too. God desires for His children to know the difference between wants and true needs. A desperate desire for a material item is a good indication of a deeper need to be accepted and understood. Ultimately, no amount of money or possessions can sustain a sacred need for purpose.

The key to finding purpose, according to Psalm 37:3–6, is to rest in God first.

> Trust in the LORD and do good;
> > dwell in the land and enjoy safe pasture.
> Take delight in the LORD,
> > and he will give you the desires of your heart.
>
> Commit your way to the LORD;
> > trust in him and he will do this:

He will make your righteous reward shine like the
dawn,
your vindication like the noonday sun.

Encourage your child to seek God and His plan instead of comparing his situation to someone else's. Take a moment to read Matthew 6:19–24 with your teen.

Do not store up for yourselves treasures on earth, where moths and vermin destroy, and where thieves break in and steal. But store up for yourselves treasures in heaven, where moths and vermin do not destroy, and where thieves do not break in and steal. For where your treasure is, there your heart will be also.

The eye is the lamp of the body. If your eyes are healthy, your whole body will be full of light. But if your eyes are unhealthy, your whole body will be full of darkness. If then the light within you is darkness, how great is that darkness!

No one can serve two masters. Either you will hate the one and love the other, or you will be devoted to the one and despise the other. You cannot serve both God and money.

Your teenager needs to discover the richness and freedom that contentment brings and have confidence that God will supply all his needs. As a parent, you may still struggle with this concept too. Don't be afraid to take an honest look at your own heart and at your family's money habits. Are there areas in which you struggle? Are there areas in which your family does really well? Prayerfully ask God to reveal these areas and help you model and teach healthy money perspectives and habits for your teenager.

As you can see, money doesn't matter when you are resting in Christ. However, it does matter when you are talking about stewardship.

> Then the word of the LORD came through the prophet Haggai: "Is it a time for you yourselves to be living in your paneled houses, while this house remains a ruin?"
>
> Now this is what the LORD Almighty says: "Give careful thought to your ways. You have planted much, but harvested little. You eat, but never have enough. You drink, but never have your fill. You put on clothes, but are not warm. You earn wages, only to put them in a purse with holes in it."
> (Hag. 1:3–6)

Money may not help us find our greater purpose, but God does care how we steward what He has entrusted to us. This passage from Haggai doesn't usually make the list of top ten verses about money, but there is a powerful message about stewardship contained in it. The prophet proclaimed God's frustration with the way His people used what had been given to them. Haggai challenged their priorities.

In this passage, the people of God were investing all their time, energy, and resources into their personal pursuits while God's house deteriorated. Even though Haggai was talking about a tangible building, it's important to remember that the temple was the symbolic home of God. His Spirit resided in the temple and was central to the spiritual lives of the Jewish people.

As New Testament believers, we are taught that God now resides within us. Although He is omnipresent, our hearts are His symbolic home. If we spend all our time, money, and energy on our own pursuits with nothing left over to build His kingdom, then His spiritual house within us lies in waste. Haggai exhorts us to examine what we have in order to redirect resources to build something meaningful and eternal.

Talking about money can be one of the most difficult discussions you will have with your teen. (Well, maybe not as challenging as discussing sex and purity!) How many times have you said to yourself or your spouse, "If I had only known then what I know now, I would've done things differently"? This year, you can be intentional about teaching your teenager the things you were never taught. By showing him a biblical view of money and the practical ways to manage it, you are blessing both your teenager and his future family.

As a parent, your financial stewardship really does count. Your teen will imitate what you do with money more than what you say about it. Regardless of how you may have struggled with money matters in the past, make every effort to practice and model good stewardship for your teen. Above all else, cultivate a spirit of thankfulness and generosity in your home—especially in the little things. By regularly infusing faith into your daily financial life, you will teach your child that God truly is the Owner and Creator of all things.

Testimony:

We actually took the Money Matters material one step further. I gave my son a bank account. I challenged him to give 10 percent and save 10 percent, but the big decision was that I told him that for his entire tenth-grade year, he was going to write the checks and pay the bills for our entire family.

I'm a single mom and handling the finances has always been my responsibility. I figured, really the only way for me to get my son prepared to be a good financier was to let him do it. We created files. We discussed the bills. This was the first time he had ever really looked at our finances. To be honest, I thought it might save me some time. Frankly, it didn't save much time. I had to sit down with him and walk him through each of the steps several times.

However, it did two things for us. First, it gave my son a new appreciation for what it takes and what it costs to run a household. Second, by the end of the year, he had figured out how to write checks on his own and save money, and he had a much better understanding of what it means to be a steward of his finances. Now that he is out of tenth grade, I had planned on resuming the responsibility of paying bills, but now we do it together, and it has become a kind of bonding experience.

A tenth grader's mom

What You Need to Know about Tenth Graders

An average tenth grader can drive a car, work a job, and is rapidly approaching adulthood. With his newfound independence, your child may express a desire to exert more control over his own life.

Dating may enter the picture more significantly this year, and if so, physical and emotional intimacy in relationships begins. Your child is still likely to exhibit impulsive behavior and be heavily influenced by his peers. Spiritually, he is much more aware of the needs of others and wants to make a difference in his world. A volunteer position at church or in the community would be an appropriate and helpful experience. With his growing social, school, and work calendar, it is likely that his need for money has increased as well. That's why this year is the ideal time to discuss money with your student.

Physically, tenth graders:

- Have a heightened sensitivity to appearance and its social value
- Have a proclivity to diet
- Are awakened sexually and are tempted to become sexually active

In addition, boys:

- Have almost completely developed into their adult bodies, though they might still grow

In addition, girls:

- Have developed physically into their adult bodies

Emotionally, tenth graders:

- Have a desire for more control over aspects of their lives
- Test authority and question rules
- Love to try new things in an effort to discover their identity
- Exhibit impulsive behavior with friends and peers
- Don't respond to adult lectures, feeling they know more about what is going on than adults
- Are more capable of taking care of others

Relationally, tenth graders:

- May begin to integrate both physical and emotional intimacy into relationships
- Seek friends who share beliefs, values, and interests
- Spend less time with family and more time with their friends
- May have peers influence them to try risky behavior such as experimenting with alcohol, tobacco, or drugs
- Prefer to compete with outside groups rather than with friends
- Negotiate with parents to get what they want

- Have a strong desire for conformity with peers
- Are strongly influenced by popular peers, adults, and celebrities

In addition, girls:

- Have a tendency to be interested in older boys

Spiritually, tenth graders:

- Can handle the responsibility of most service positions in the church
- Have a greater interest in serving others and in making a difference in the world
- Begin planning and preparation for the future
- Are better able to identify right and wrong
- Choose role models who inspire them either toward or away from faith
- Have increased capacity for self-discipline
- Are spiritually influenced through summer camps and mission experiences because of the peer connections those events create
- Begin to imagine what life would be like as an adult away from their parents and begin deciding whether their faith will be a part of their future
- Are tempted to have fun now and be responsible later

12

Eleventh Grade: Family Tree

Your teenager is more than halfway through high school now. In less than two years, she will begin her life as an adult. Whether you have worked your way through the rites of passage since kindergarten or are starting this year, you can never underestimate the power of infusing faith into your family.

The Bible says that our spiritual influence continues to the third and fourth generation. That makes you, as a parent, a spiritual patriarch or matriarch in your family's legacy. Pretty daunting, isn't it? The influence you have and the path you mark out will have an effect on your grandchildren, your great-grandchildren, and even your great-great-grandchildren. What you do today matters! Before your child becomes a senior and then moves out to start her own life and eventually her own family, you have the opportunity to teach her about her heritage. You can help her understand where she came from and where she is going, and in doing so, your spiritual legacy will expand and deepen.

Eleventh Grade Rite of Passage
Ceremony: Family-tree dinner
Symbol: Family heirloom

The eleventh grade Rite of Passage Experience is to plan a family-tree dinner. The important part of the dinner is not cooking an elaborate meal for your entire clan but empowering your teenager to investigate, discover, and report on her family heritage.

The first step in planning the event is to review the Family Interview Questions found in the Resource section and give them to your teenager. She will then contact and interview at least three family members outside of your immediate family. Their answers can be documented on paper, with a voice recorder, or even with a video camera. How the interview is done is far less important than what she learns from interviewing.

The results of the interviews will be presented at the family event you plan with your teenager. It can be a dinner, a trip to visit family in another town or state, or a full-blown family reunion. If gathering with family isn't possible, consider using video-conferencing technology or recording the presentation to share at a later date or via mail. This is your family, so you can determine what will work best.

Sometime before the event, sit down with your teenager and let her share with you what she learned in her family-member interviews. Help her edit the interviews to make them ready to present to other family members. While interviewing family members, your teen may have learned family secrets or other things that may not be appropriate to share in a group setting, and you can discuss these things with her. Understanding family issues that she was previously too young to know about is an important part of learning the history of the family, so be sure to allow plenty of time for conversation.

At the appointed time, gather the family together. You can begin the family-tree dinner by giving a State of the Family address, in which you remind your family of who they are, affirm their identities, and offer a blessing. Let your teenager speak next and report what she learned. After she shares, you can open the floor to other family members to share their own memories, encourage your eleventh grader, or simply share their hearts. This has the potential to be a powerful moment for your family and for your teen.

At the conclusion of the family event, you can present your teen with a family heirloom. This can be something significant that was passed down to you, or you can start a new tradition with a gift that has special meaning to your child. You also might want to ask older family members for ideas concerning the family heirloom. They might surprise you with something you didn't even know existed. If you are still struggling with ideas for a family heirloom, consider these questions:

- What budget do I have for a family heirloom?
- What do I own that has special meaning to me?
- What can I give that is durable enough to last for generations?
- What would symbolize our family's mission statement?
- What symbol can I give that would demonstrate our family's emphasis on faith?

Before you close the evening with a time of blessings and prayer for your child, you may want to ask each person to share what they are thankful for. The point of the rite of passage is to invite your teenager to something greater than herself. The family-tree dinner helps her understand that she is part of a family and a faith that are bigger than she is.

Testimony:

I never enjoyed visiting my great-grandfather as a teenager. It's not that he was a mean person. He was actually really kind to me. He always sent me birthday cards, and whenever I was around, he would light up. I guess he just seemed boring to me.

One day, I was dreading an upcoming visit, so I tried to come up with a plan to make the visit less boring. I realized in that moment that I knew nothing about my great-grandfather. That day, I began to ask him some simple questions. You know what I learned? My great-grandfather used to be the mayor of the town in which he lived. He also worked for the company that made the atomic bomb. Isn't that amazing?

Over the following weeks and years, he spun tales that made me buckle over in laughter and some that made me sad. I remember when he told me how he fell in love with his wife and how much it hurt him when she died. My grandfather had so much to share, and it has helped me figure a lot of things out. I learned that the first step to knowing who you are is to discover where you came from.

                                    Young man reflecting on his eleventh-grade year

Resource

Family interview questions

- What is the greatest thing you have ever learned in life?
- What or who has been the greatest influence in your life?
- Do you have a favorite scripture? If so, what is it?
- What are your beliefs about God?
- Can you tell me about your parents and your relationship with them?
- One day I might be a parent. What advice would you have for me as a parent?
- How did you meet your spouse? Can you tell me about how you fell in love?
- Based on your experience in marriage, what advice would you give me about love and marriage?
- Tell me about your career. How did you choose it, and where did you get your start?
- What advice would you give me about work that you have learned through your career?
- What significant historical event do you remember the most that happened in your lifetime?

- If you could live your life all over again, what would you do differently?
- Where is the best place you have ever traveled?
- What is the best movie you have ever seen?
- What is the best book you have ever read?
- How do you want people to remember you?

Laying the Foundation of Faith

> Finally, all of you, be like-minded, be sympathetic, love one another, be compassionate and humble. Do not repay evil with evil or insult with insult. On the contrary, repay evil with blessing, because to this you were called so that you may inherit a blessing. (1 Pet. 3:8–9)

Each person in your family plays a role in influencing the others. Between birth-order tendencies, gender differences, and personality traits, your family has an impact on how you see and respond to the world. God calls us to be deeply rooted in Him and with each other, because deep roots produce strength, fruit, and shelter for generations.

> These are the visions I saw while lying in bed: I looked, and there before me stood a tree in the middle of the land. Its height was enormous. The tree grew large and strong and its top touched the sky; it was visible to the ends of the earth. Its

leaves were beautiful, its fruit abundant, and on it
was food for all. Under it the wild animals found
shelter, and the birds lived in its branches; from it
every creature was fed. (Dan. 4:10–12)

The tree Daniel saw in his dream in the passage above was a
magnificent sight. It was strong and beautiful. What makes it a
remarkable tree was not just what it looked like, though, but also
what it produced—fruit, shelter, and a place to gather. What an
amazing metaphor for a strong family. Use this verse to evaluate your
family tree. Does your family have anything in common with this
magnificent tree? What is missing in your family tree that is depicted
in this scripture? What small or big things could help your family
produce the kind of fruit and shelter this tree provides? Spend some
time asking God this question, and then listen for His response.

In addition to fruit and shelter, deeply rooted families can also
withstand the powerful storms of life.

The promise is for you and your children and for
all who are far off—for all whom the Lord our God
will call. (Acts 2:39)

Has his unfailing love vanished forever?
    Has his promise failed for all time? (Ps. 77:8)

For the LORD is good and his love endures forever;
    his faithfulness continues through all
        generations. (Ps. 100:5)

No family tree is perfect. Sometimes people within the family are responsible for making things messy; other times tragedy, which seems to have no perpetrator, strikes. The key to maintaining deep roots in a broken world is to actively trust that God wants to bless your siblings, grandkids, great-nephews, long-lost third cousins twice removed, and every other relative through the promises in His Word. Those you love may be far from God, but He still knows where they are and His arm of grace extends there. You may have endured terrible storms and were bent to the point of breaking, but you can hold on to the promise that His loving-kindness keeps you from being uprooted.

When those kinds of storms happen during your child's turbulent adolescent years, it can threaten the roots you have so carefully tended. Honest encounters with grief, disappointment, grace, forgiveness, conflict, and restoration will help your teen trust God's promises and see His hand at work.

By choosing to infuse faith into your daily rhythm of life, you are cultivating deep family roots. Consider the following questions.

- What's my job in the spiritual community of my family?
- How will I do that job well in my relationships with siblings and parents?
- What does it mean to be called to live a certain way?
- How can that make a difference in my family?

Try to identify ways to be more deeply rooted in your family. Here are a few to get you started:

- Do family reviews. Reminisce about fun times and retell stories that bring a smile.
- Sibling rivalries are obviously normal, but continue to play a role in refereeing teachable moments.
- Encourage your teen to make a coupon book of activities and treats she is willing to redeem for a younger sibling.
- Eat dinner together often. This is a lost family art in our busy lives.
- Cook with your teen and let her pick the recipe to tackle.
- Work in the yard or cultivate a garden together.
- Show up for each other's big stuff. There's nothing like a family cheering section!

The story of your family is your unique story. It's the place you belong, and it brings you identity. One of the best ways you can help your eleventh grader embrace her identity is to help her discover your family's heritage. Whether the story of your family is a page-turning novel, a comedy sketch, or even if it reads like a police report, your teenager needs to hear the good, the bad, and the ultimate redemption that Christ brings to every family. What an amazing opportunity to inscribe your family's story of faith on the heart of your child.

What You Need to Know about Eleventh Graders

By the time your teenager reaches the eleventh-grade year, her life seems like that of a miniadult. However, no matter how mature she seems or independent she acts, she still needs your guidance. Stress may become a real problem this year as she struggles to balance work, school, social life, and making future plans and big decisions. She may even become sentimental as she anticipates the coming changes. Her friend group more closely aligns with her values and activities as her time and focus narrow. Church activities and family traditions are also important, although she may not want to admit it.

Physically, eleventh graders:

- Have fully developed into their adult bodies
- Are awakened sexually and are tempted to become sexually active
- Become more physically stressed as they work, perform in school, and prepare for the future

Emotionally, eleventh graders:

- Become very sentimental as they anticipate life's changes
- Experience calmer moods than in previous years

- Have a desire for more control over aspects of their lives
- Exhibit impulsive behavior with friends and peers
- Don't respond to adult lectures, feeling they know more about what is going on than adults
- Are more capable of taking care of others

Relationally, eleventh graders:

- Begin to integrate both physical and emotional intimacy into relationships
- Seek friends who share the same beliefs, values, and interests
- Spend less time with family and more time with their friends
- May have peers influence them to try risky behaviors, such as experimenting with alcohol, tobacco, or drugs
- Develop relationships with parents as more of a support system
- Begin to feel freedom to express themselves as individuals

Spiritually, eleventh graders:

- Value the annual traditions of their student ministries, churches, and families in regard to faith

- Can handle the responsibility of most service positions in the church
- Have a greater interest in serving others and in making a difference in the world
- Plan and prepare for the future
- Choose role models who inspire them either toward or away from faith
- Have increased capacity for self-discipline
- Begin to imagine what life would be like as an adult away from their parents and begin deciding whether their faith will be a part of that
- Are tempted to have fun now and be responsible later

13

Twelfth Grade: Manhood/ Womanhood Ceremony

A few years ago, I (Jeremy) was invited to a special evening of blessing for an eighteen-year-old. The young man's father asked a few of the men who had been influential in his son's life to attend and share some words of encouragement with him. After the men finished sharing, the father took center stage and an amazing thing happened. He asked his son to kneel down on the floor in front of him. He walked over to the hallway closet, opened the door, and brought out a huge *Braveheart*-style sword, purchased just for the evening. He laid the sword on the son's shoulder and said something I will never forget: "Son, I know many thirty- and forty-year-old men who act like children because no one ever told them that they were men. Tonight, on your eighteenth birthday, based on the authority of God's Word that He has given me, I say to you that you knelt down as a boy, but you will rise as a man."

While certainly unconventional, it was one of the most power- ful parenting moments I have ever witnessed. When the young man stood up, he stood with pride. He was a man because his dad said he was. In that moment, the blessing was unleashed.

When I (Jim) used to speak for the Promise Keepers organization, Randy Phillips, their president at the time, used to always say, "A man is not a man until his father tells him he is." This concept is equally true for young women, that they are not women until their mothers say they are.

Your child is entering his senior year of high school. This is the grand finale of your parenting journey. At this crossroad in your child's life, you have a chance to hold up a figurative mirror to his soul and give him a glimpse of who God created him to be. When you unleash your blessing as a parent, you're releasing your teenager to change the world. Who wouldn't want to give that kind of blessing to their child?

Twelfth Grade Rite of Passage
Ceremony: Manhood/womanhood ceremony
Symbol: Gift to commemorate the moment

The twelfth grade Rite of Passage Experience allows you to exercise your biblical authority to proclaim to your teenager that he is now an adult. This ceremony represents the end of the final chapter in the story of your teenager's childhood and adolescence. It's a chance for you to launch your child into the world armed with an understanding of who God made him to be.

Begin your planning by talking with your teenager about this special occasion. Let him have a say in the format and location of the ceremony. Would he prefer a small, intimate gathering or a huge party? Is there going to be a formal dinner or a casual dessert? Ask him to make a list of the people who have been influential in his life, then use it as the guest list for the ceremony. When you invite attendees to be a part of the occasion, ask them to prepare a special word of encouragement for your teenager—including their understanding of being a man or a woman of God.

Take time to think about and pray through what you want to communicate, and prepare an agenda for the ceremony well in advance. Plan time for the guests to share, choose some favorite or meaningful scriptures to read, and write or type your remarks. Make sure you include an announcement of your teenager's departure from childhood into adulthood and a prayer of blessing. You might also want to give him a symbol to help him remember the night you declared him to be an adult. (For help in planning the evening, review the planning guide in the Resource section.)

Above all, risk vulnerability. If the ceremony is cold or unfeeling, it won't be effective or meaningful. However, it will be a significant moment if you open your heart, hold up a mirror to your child's soul, and share what you see as his identity in Christ.

Resources

Planning guide for the ceremony

- Discuss the ceremony with your twelfth grader. Should it be private, public, formal, or casual? He can help choose the format, but he can't choose whether or not he will receive the blessing at the ceremony.

- Decide whom to invite and send them not only the details of the evening, but give them an idea of what you expect them to share with your twelfth grader at the ceremony. That will give them time to prepare.

- Be ready for questions. Your teenager might see this as strange or awkward, which is actually pretty typical. It will be something that will be more easily understood when experienced. Learn to be comfortable with questions and use the answer, "You'll have to just wait and see" a lot.

- Prepare to give your child a symbol. Decide what you will give him and what meaning you are going to attach to it. If you can, try to make this a surprise for your twelfth grader, which will make it even more fun.

- Write down what you plan to say. Not only will it calm your nerves to read it, but you can also give a written copy of it to your teenager as a keepsake.

- Bless your child's identity, not his performance.

- Be creative. Every ceremony is completely different because it is for a unique child of God and comes from the hearts and minds of the parents who are leading it.

- Pray. Give all the guests an opportunity to pray over your teenager.

- Read some scriptures of blessing. See the Scripture Blessings resource section for ideas.

Scripture blessings

Here is a list of possible scriptures you can read during the manhood/womanhood ceremony.

Isaiah 49:25	Proverbs 4:18	Deuteronomy 6:7
Isaiah 44:3–4	Proverbs 4:22	Proverbs 1:8–9
Psalm 112:2	Psalm 119:11	Psalm 128:1–6
Psalm 127:3	Jeremiah 32:38–39	Hebrews 12:9–11
Isaiah 54:13	Zechariah 9:11	1 Peter 2:9
1 Corinthians 13:11	Psalm 91	Genesis 18:19
Proverbs 20:7	Psalm 144:12	Jeremiah 1:5
Numbers 6:24	Psalm 127:3–5	Psalm 127:1
Proverbs 27:11	Psalm 139:13–16	Proverbs 23:24
2 Timothy 2:22	Proverbs 22:6	Joshua 1:6–15
Proverbs 2:20	Ephesians 6:4	Romans 8:28
Proverbs 4:8	Jeremiah 29:11	
(good for woman-		
hood ceremony)		

Ideas for releasing a person of true identity in Christ

- Make college visits and intentionally discuss what God can do in your child's life at each school.
- Have lunch or dinner one-on-one weekly during his senior year.

- Ask five adults who are significant in your teen's life to pray for his future throughout the year.
- Encourage your teen to find a mentor during the first semester of college.
- Make sure your teen knows how to do laundry and how to change a tire. (Really!)
- Ask your teen what he needs from you during his senior year in order to finish well.

Blessing script to read during the ceremony

If your twelfth grader has made the decision to follow Christ with his life, you have a special opportunity to offer a spiritual blessing during the manhood/womanhood ceremony. The following is a blessing written by my (Jeremy's) spiritual mentor, Dr. Ed Laymance. Thousands of families have used the biblical truths in this writing to remind their children of their identity in Christ. We hope you find it useful as you conduct this important rite of passage with your teen.

"I Am a Child of the King" by Dr. Ed Laymance

Because of who Jesus Christ is, and
    because He is my Savior and
    my Lord:
I am a child of the King of Kings and   (Rev. 1:8, John 1:12)
    Lord of Lords,

seated with Christ in the heavenly realm. I   (Eph. 2:6, I Pet. 2:9)
am chosen, accepted,

and included—a citizen of heaven   (John 14:1–6, Eph. 2:19)
and a member of God's
household.

I am loved by God unconditionally and   (Rom. 5:6–8, I John 4:10)
without reservation.

I belong to Him, having been bought by   (I Peter 2:9, I Cor. 6:19)
Him with the

precious blood of Jesus. I have eternal life   (I John 5:11–13, John 3:16)
and will be

saved from all of God's wrath to   (Rom. 5:9, Eph. 1:13–14)
come—guaranteed!

I am a Christian. I am not just different in   (I Peter 4:16)
what I do.

My identity has changed. Who I am has   (II Cor. 5:17, Gal. 2:20)
changed. Everything has
become brand new.

I am a dwelling place in which God lives   (Eph. 2:22, I Cor. 6:19)
by His Spirit.

I have access to Him anytime, anywhere,   (Eph. 2:18, Phil. 4:6–7)
for any reason.

I am God's creation—His workmanship. I   (Ps. 139, Eph. 2:10)
was created by Him

and for Him, so who I am and what I do   (Col. 1:16, Gal. 6:7-9)
matters.

I am spiritually alive. I have been set free   (Rom. 6:8-11, Heb. 2:14–15)
from the fear of death

and have been given life to live and enjoy   (John 10:10)
     to the full.

I am forgiven—completely, totally, and   (I John 1:9, Ps. 103:8–13)
     absolutely.

I have been rescued from the dominion of
     darkness and

brought into the Kingdom of light—the   (Col. 1:13)
     Kingdom of the Son.

I have been set free from the penalty of sin   (Rom. 6:16-23, Gal. 5:1)
     and the power of sin.

I am an enemy of Satan and at war with   (I Pet. 5:8, Eph. 6:12)
     spiritual forces of evil, but

greater is He that is in me than he that is   (I John 4:4)
     in the world.

If God is for me, it doesn't matter who or   (Rom. 8:31, Eph. 1:18–23)
     what stands against me,

because nothing and no one can separate
     me from the love of Christ—

not hurt, pain, loss, problem, or
     brokenness;

not persecution, trouble, difficulty, or
     danger;

not abandonment, abuse, addictions, or
     appetites;

not desires, food, sexuality, or
     relationships;

not life or death, angels or demons;

not my past, the present, or the future;

no power, no person, no place, not   (Rom. 8:35–39)
      anything in all creation;
not even Satan himself shall prevail.   (Col. 2:15)
I am in the hands of Jesus, in the hands of
      God, and nothing and
no one can snatch me out of God's hands.   (John 10:27–28)
I will fear no evil because God is with   (Ps. 23:4, II Tim. 1:7)
      me, and
He has promised to never leave me nor   (Heb. 13:5)
      forsake me.
God's presence is with me everywhere   (Ps. 139:7)
      I go—
to the heights of heaven,
through the valley of the shadow,
to the ends of the earth—forever and   (Matt. 28:19–20)
      always.
I am a child of the King and choose this
      day to live as one.

Laying the Foundation of Faith

Your parenting skills have been honed over the last eighteen years, but they are about to be tested. Your child's transition from dependence on you to independence comes to a jarring climax during his senior year. The reality that the baby you once held will soon live a life separate from yours can be overwhelming. In fact, for a lot of parents, this season is harder on them than on their kids. Some parents react by smothering or overparenting their child. As you can imagine, this response only serves to push most teens further away. Helping your teen make the transition from childhood to adulthood can be complicated and confusing, but don't worry! Give yourself grace, and realize that your behavior is probably rooted in the fear of letting go instead of trusting God to take care of your child. The best way to remind yourself of His faithfulness is to turn to His Word.

> When I consider your heavens,
>   the work of your fingers,
> the moon and the stars,
>   which you have set in place,
> what is mankind that you are mindful of them,
>   human beings that you care for them?
> You have made them a little lower than the angels
>   and crowned them with glory and honor.
>   (Ps. 8:3–5)

In high school, the questions your senior will be most frequently asked are, "Where are you going to college?" and "Have you chosen a major?" and "What do you want to do with your life?" While none of these questions is inherently the wrong question, none of them is the most important one. Rather than asking him what he wants to do, the best question to ask is, "Who do you want to become?"

Chances are good that a college degree will not be in the same field as the graduate's ultimate profession. Statistics say the average person changes careers every seven years. Why set your child up for a crisis by basing his identity on what he chooses to study? Help him shape his future plans by basing them on whose he is! Your teenager is a child of God who was created to do good works for His kingdom. If he learns to embrace this truth, no matter where his feet land, he will never question his purpose or identity.

God loves to surprise His children with plans different from the ones they had in mind.

> As Jesus walked beside the Sea of Galilee, he saw Simon and his brother Andrew casting a net into the lake, for they were fishermen. "Come, follow me," Jesus said, "and I will send you out to fish for people." (Mark 1:16–17)

This may be one of the most difficult truths for parents to accept. Most parents feel better when their kids have a normal, "safe" plan for their lives. But the road to a deep faith in Jesus is often unpredictable and faith filled. He frequently calls His children to step out of their comfort zones.

God calls you to trust His plans, not your own. Your teen will continue to build a healthy identity if you help him answer the question, "Who do I want to become?" Help him make a list of answers to that question, and then show him you aren't afraid to wade into the answers he gives.

The final test of your teen's spiritual readiness to move into adulthood is whether he can answer two questions, one vertical and one horizontal. First, Is your vertical relationship with the Creator and Savior the most important love you ever give away? Second, Do you know how to give the same love that flows from your vertical relationship with God to your horizontal relationships with others?

Your greatest desire for your teen should be that he loves others as God has fully and wholeheartedly loved him.

> Jesus replied: "'Love the Lord your God with all your heart and with all your soul and with all your mind.' This is the first and greatest command-ment. And the second is like it: 'Love your neighbor as yourself.' All the Law and the Prophets hang on these two commandments." (Matt. 22:37–40)

One of the greatest privileges God gives to us parents is the ability to release our children into adulthood. If you are wondering whether it's significant, consider your own life. Was there a time when your parents gave you a blessing and affirmed you as an adult? If so, be thankful. If not, how would having such as blessing have changed your perspective? How would it have influenced your decisions, your confidence, and your navigation into adult life? Now you have the opportunity to influence all those things for your teenager.

This is your last Rite of Passage Experience. Take a deep breath, say a prayer, and maybe even shed a tear. It's time to complete the journey. Well done!

Testimony:

As I look back at key moments of my life, a manhood ceremony that my parents put together for me has to rank as one of my best experiences. When they first told me about the ceremony, I thought it was pretty lame. It sounded more for the adults than for me. However, on the day of the ceremony, my parents worked really hard at creating a great meal with a festive atmosphere. I still wasn't sure how I felt about it. Then people in my life who were important to me started arriving. I was surprised to see my baseball coach and his wife. My youth pastor came. It seemed like all of my family and extended family.

The atmosphere was fun. It was like a party. Then my dad called everyone together and he had me sit in a chair. He told the people that anyone who wanted to participate could do so, but it had to be brief. Many of the people had written out their words of affirmation and encouragement. It was really moving and I even find myself crying as I write these words. Each person came from a different perspective. Then my mom and dad handed me an heirloom family Bible and said it was now mine. They asked me to kneel and said something like, "You have knelt down as a boy, but you will rise as a man." There was lots of hugging and some tears, but it is an experience I will never forget and hope to do with my children when I have them.

A newly married husband reflecting on his senior year of high school

What You Need to Know about Twelfth Graders

For all practical purposes, your twelfth grader is a grown-up. Physically, most seventeen-to-eighteen-year-olds have completely developed into their adult bodies, but your adult child still needs your encouragement and support. Stress continues to be a real struggle, as college applications, senior events, and a demanding schedule take their tolls. Because the most common question posed to your child is, "Do you know where you are going to college?" it can be especially stress-inducing if he hasn't decided where to go yet or if he even plans to go at all. Try to maintain a positive and encouraging stance as he confronts issues of faith, his future, and his relationships. He may show less interest in student ministry, but only because he is ready to be connected to more mature faith discussions.

Physically, twelfth graders:

- Have developed into their adult bodies
- Are awakened sexually and are tempted to become sexually active
- Become more physically stressed as they work, perform in school, and prepare for the future

Emotionally, twelfth graders:

- Begin to be very sentimental as they anticipate life's changes
- Experience calmer moods than in previous years
- Exhibit impulsive behavior with friends and peers
- Are more capable of taking care of others

Relationally, twelfth graders:

- Integrate both physical and emotional intimacy into relationships
- Seek friends who share the same beliefs, values, and interests

- Develop relationships with parents as more of a support system
- Begin to feel freedom to express themselves as individuals

Spiritually, twelfth graders:

- Can handle the responsibility of most service positions in the church
- Have much less interest in student ministry activities and need to be connected to adult activities in the church
- Have a greater interest in serving others and making a difference in the world
- Choose role models who inspire them either toward or away from faith
- Are tempted to have fun now and be responsible later

Part 3

Finish Strong

Crossing the Finish Line

This may seem hard, but we want you to imagine your child as a grandparent.

She has gray hair, walks far slower than she does now, and has a bunch of really cute grandkids gathered around her.

Now let's imagine one of those grandkids looks up at her and asks, "What was it like when you were growing up?"

What will your grown child think, feel, and say when she reflects on what she learned in your home?

Do you accept the role God has given you as a spiritual patriarch or matriarch of your family for the next three to four generations? Then it's that picture that should drive the way you parent every day.

Imagine that moment when your grown child follows your lead and begins to share with your grandchildren the beauty of Jesus Christ. This is very possible, but it won't happen by accident. We've got to harness the power of shared experiences to strategically pass down faith.

When your child looks back on what she learned from you, her reflection will be marked by the moments and memories you shared as a family. Perhaps your child will talk about the vacations you enjoyed, a crisis you endured together, or the traditions that took place around the holidays in your home.

As parents, we often rely on lectures to get our points across, but kids don't remember lectures as much as they remember a *shared experience*.

It's true that a lot of the experiences we share with our kids are not planned, and they are certainly not all pleasant. In fact, you could put a lot of work into planning a shared experience and be really disappointed by your child's ho-hum reaction to it. But none of those things should stop you from trying. One of the most powerful ways to guide and teach your child is through being intentional about making memories together. The heart of this book is to inspire you to leverage the power in your home.

It is possible to plan an event with your child that has real meaning for both of you. It is possible to think creatively and make a memory together through a shared experience that is not just fun but also passes down an understanding of what matters most in life.

So our encouragement today is that you get out a piece of paper and start dreaming, planning, and preparing for a shared experience with your child that has the potential to change her life.

This is the heart behind the Rites of Passage Experiences. You might not do any of the experiences you have read about in this book. But if you start to think creatively and strategically about shared spiritual experiences you can create in your home, we have done our job.

In Massillon, Ohio, a town of about thirty thousand people, the president of the booster club visits every male baby born in the city and gives him a small football with the high school football team's logo on it. He says to the new mom, "On behalf of Massillon High School, we want to congratulate you on your new Tiger, and we look forward to the day that he plays for our football team."

That little baby is wearing diapers the size of an adult's elbow, and he is already being recruited to play football! What is that? That is a high school football program that decided to be strategic. And it just might be why they have won twenty-two state championships.

There is something powerful in stepping back and making a plan to do things on purpose. Since parenting is one of the most important things you or I will ever do, we should be strategic in our parenting. You either received healthy and strategic guidance from your parents growing up or you didn't. If you had great, strategic, and healthy parents pouring into your life growing up, you know how valuable it is. We don't have to convince you of the importance of repeating that in the life of your child. Perhaps you didn't have a great experience with your parents growing up, though, and you were left wanting so much more. You didn't get what you needed, and that left you as an adult having to fend for yourself. We don't have to say anything to you about how hard it is when a child is forced to learn life by herself without help from her parents. You, possibly more than those who grew up with great spiritual influencers as parents, know how vital it is to pass down a godly legacy to your children; you want to give them what you lacked in your home of origin.

Let's consider the Rites of Passage Experiences we have explored in this book:

- Kindergarten: An Invitation to Generosity
- First Grade: An Invitation to Responsibility
- Second Grade: An Invitation to the Bible
- Third Grade: An Invitation to Rhythm
- Fourth Grade: An Invitation to Friendship

- Fifth Grade: An Invitation to Identity
- Sixth Grade: Preparing for Adolescence
- Seventh Grade: The Blessing
- Eighth Grade: Purity Code Weekend
- Ninth Grade: Driving Contract
- Tenth Grade: Money Matters
- Eleventh Grade: Family Tree
- Twelfth Grade: Manhood/Womanhood Ceremony

Did you receive all thirteen of these conversations and experiences from your parents in a healthy way when you were growing up? We've asked thousands of parents, and no one has ever raised his or her hand. We can't raise our hands either.

Do you see the power of being strategic? If all you do is just one of these Rites of Passage Experiences each year, you will have given your child more than most adults have ever received.

We'd like to end with our own blessing for you and your family.

May God bless your family.

May God keep your family firmly in His hand.

May God unleash His presence in your home and pursue passionately you and all your children.

May you and your children learn, love, and live God's Word daily.

May God seal your hearts with His love and His truth.

May God give you a vision and a passion for passing down faith in your home.

Notes

Part 1
Chapter 1—A Legacy Moment

1. Jim Burns, *Faith Conversations for Families* (Ventura, CA: Regal/Gospel Light, 2011), 7.

2. Mark Merrill, "A Father's Legacy," *Mark Merrill: Helping Families Love Well,* June 14, 2010, www.markmerrill.com/a-fathers-legacy.

3. "The State of Vacation Bible School," Barna Group, July 9, 2013, www .barna.org/barna-update/family-kids/619-the-state-of-vacation-bible-school# .VIdQ-JZ0zcs.

Part 2
Chapter 4—Third Grade: An Invitation to Rhythm

1. *Merriam-Webster Online*, s.v. "rhythm," accessed May 6, 2015, www.merriam -webster.com/dictionary/rhythm.

Chapter 6—Fifth Grade: An Invitation to Identity

1. *Wikipedia*, s.v. "Erikson's Stages of Psychosocial Development," last modified May 5, 2015, https://en.wikipedia.org/wiki/Erikson%27s_stages_of _psychosocial_development.

2. *Merriam-Webster Online*, s.v. "identity," accessed May 6, 2015, www.merriam -webster.com/dictionary/identity.

Chapter 9—Eighth Grade: Purity Code Weekend

1. The Pure Foundation Series has many valuable books, including *Teaching Your Children Healthy Sexuality*, *God Made Your Body*, *How God Makes Babies*, and *Accept Nothing Less*, and is available online at www.HomeWord.com, https://homeword.com/product-category/pure-foundation-series/.

2. In no way have we tried to cover all the important subjects of sex education for your child in this one Purity Code Weekend Rite of Passage Experience. All experts in the field of sex education challenge parents to understand that healthy sex education is an ongoing discussion and dialogue that begins much earlier than the eighth grade and often continues until the wedding. These same experts tell us that the more positive, healthy sex education kids receive from home, the less promiscuous they will be. With the Purity Code Weekend rite of passage celebration, we have actually raised the bar to challenge your child to commit to a high standard of sexual integrity and purity. We are very much aware that some young people will become vulnerable to temptation and make poor decisions in this area. We want to add here that if your kids do violate their values in this area, make sure that along with important dialogue, and perhaps some consequences, you surround your child with the grace and love that God Himself gives those who fall short of His standards. We think a very good resource for this age group is a book Jim Burns wrote titled *The Purity Code: God's Plan for Sex and Your Body* (Bloomington, MN: Bethany, 2008).

3. Pure Foundation Series.

4. "Statistics on Pornography, Sexual Addiction and Online Perpetrators," TechMission Safe Families, www.safefamilies.org/sfStats.php.

5. For more in-depth information about sexuality and how to discuss it with your child, check out *Teaching Your Children Healthy Sexuality* by Jim Burns (Bloomington, MN: Bethany, 2008).

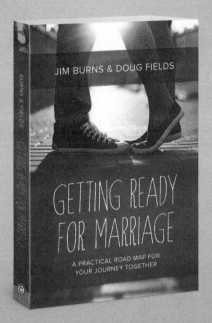

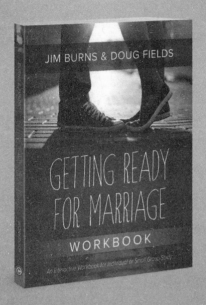

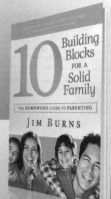
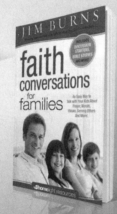